Warriors of the Ultimate Fighting™ Championship®

Warriors

of the
Ultimate Fighting™
Championship®

ERICH KRAUSS

CITADEL PRESS
Kensington Publishing Corp.
www.kensingtonbooks.com

CITADEL PRESS BOOKS are published by

Kensington Publishing Corp.
850 Third Avenue
New York, NY 10022

First printing: November 2004

10 9 8 7 6 5 4 3 2 1

Printed in the United States of America

Library of Congress Control Number: 2004109742

ISBN 0-8065-2657-2

Special Thanks

To Joe Silva and Jack Taylor, who have done a tremendous amount of editing and re-writing.

To Josh Hedges, who shot all of the photographs (which are owned and copyrighted by Zuffa, LLC), and who also designed and created the graphics and artwork on the cover.

Also, thanks to Donna Spaulding, secretary to Dana White.

Contents

SECTION THREE

The Strikers

Foreword

The Ultimate Fighting Championship:
The Great Savior of the Art of Fighting

by Joe Rogan

I've been heavily involved in marital arts since the age of fourteen. I started out with kenpo karate, then eventually went to tae kwon do, always looking for the best "style" of fighting art. This was somewhere around 1982, and there was a lot of confusion and debate back then regarding styles. Everyone was supposed to be loyal to the style they practiced, and we were even admonished for practicing outside of our chosen art.

There were a lot of closed-minded, insecure instructors back then, and often they were more concerned with keeping their enrollment high than they were with advancing the progress of martial arts. They taught that everything that was effective was contained within the style that they had chosen to practice, and that practitioners of all other styles were enemies.

There was always debate as to what would happen if a karate guy fought a judo guy, who would win if a boxer got in the ring with a Muay Thai fighter, and so on, ad nauseam. Every style thought that it had the advantage, and until 1993 the subject was open to debate.

In 1993 the martial arts finally got out of the dark ages of ignorance and insecurity with the birth of the Ultimate Fighting Championship (UFC).

The debate was over. The world was given a chance to see a skinny man from South America named Royce Gracie strangle everyone in front of him en route to taking the championship and to turning traditional martial arts on its side.

I remember hearing about the UFC back then and thinking, "Wow. Someone finally did it." They finally had a tournament to see what style is the most effective. They put them all together and in a cage to boot. I didn't know if it was just a one-time thing or if it was going to be a regular event.

I talked to some guys at the gym about it, and they all had different thoughts. "Yeah, this skinny dude from Argentina or something beat everyone. He did some kind of judo and choked everyone."

I remember being skeptical. I thought, "A judo guy beat everyone? Maybe he got lucky. Shit happens in tournaments. People get injured, and sometimes the best guy doesn't win." I finally located a copy of the tournament at my local video store. It was actually the second UFC tournament, and I watched in awe as Gracie again effortlessly ran the table. That was no luck, I thought. That's the real shit, right there. Gracie knew exactly what he was doing, and his opponents were completely ignorant of his moves. The whole event was completely eye opening, and it forever changed the way I looked at fighting.

I watched the ferocious Pat Smith completely demolish Scott Morris in the most brutal display of "real fighting" I had ever seen. The two men locked up in one of the most famous beat downs in the history of what's now known as mixed martial arts (MMA). The kickboxer Smith mounted the Ninjitsu stylist Morris and delivered a series of vicious elbows down onto Morris's head, instantly splattering blood all over his face, completely separating him from his consciousness, and completely separating traditional martial artists from their illusions of invulnerability.

The notions of "death touches" and how they could use "chi" to avoid being harmed in battle were finally considered appropriately ridiculous. There it was right in front of our eyes; a real live Ninja master was down on his face smashed into pulp. No death touch, no chi, just a vicious beat down that he didn't have the skills or the knowledge to prevent. It was the beginning of a completely new sport, the purest form of all sports: mixed martial arts.

With each UFC event new lessons were learned; Gracie showed the beauty of the grappling art of jiu-jitsu and of how a much smaller man could dominate a larger, stronger foe with superior technique. Marco Ruas taught us the effectiveness of leg kicks. Maurice Smith showed how a striker could beat a grappler with superior fitness and strategy. Vitor Belfort, a fighter with both ground skills and vicious striking, showed the world a scary new combination. Fighters were advancing and evolving rapidly, and competitors who were at one time known for a single discipline were now developing skills in all areas: kickboxers were winning fights by submission and wrestlers were winning fights by knockout.

The playing field was made more level with the adoption of weight classes and the implementation of new rules: head butts were disallowed and rounds were made shorter to allow fighters to compete at a more aggressive pace. The evolution has been so rapid that you can see the progress clearly by just comparing an event of five years ago with one of today.

And the truly fascinating thing is that for a good portion of this time the sport was banned from cable television in the United States. All this evolution and growth occurred while the sport was only available to pay-per-view satellite television and only discussed on the Internet.

No mainstream news coverage and no free television airings were available, but the sport continued to grow and evolve. Can that be said of any other sport today?

The appeal of it can be clearly demonstrated by how openly it's been embraced by the Japanese, whose culture is far more accepting of all things martial. In Japan, with no resistance or censorship by cable or pay-per-view, their events fill massive arenas and their fighters are huge mainstream celebrities. The number-one event in Japan, PRIDE, has had shows with as many as 90,000 people in attendance and millions watching on television.

Although there hasn't been a single death or serious injury in the ten years that the UFC has been around, there are still people in the United States who find it barbaric and believe it should be banned. Why? Because it's just too real.

There are many people who don't wish to be reminded about the true nature of man. We're okay with the hundreds of deaths that have occurred over the years in high school football because those are unfortunate accidents. NASCAR can show fiery wrecks on national television that leave the drivers permanently disfigured or dead, but again, those are accidents, so we accept them. Actually watching a man purposely attacking another with skill and determination is just too much for them, even if it's statistically far safer than "accepted" sports. It's just too raw for people who like to view the world with rose-colored glasses to watch competition on its base level. The reality of the nature of man is that as long as there is testosterone and the will to procreate, there will always be fighting.

Some of it will be done on the stock market floor, some of it will be done on the basketball court, and some of it will be done in the court of law—but make no mistake about it, at its root level, it's all just fighting. It's male domination.

The chimpanzee DNA is looking to establish its host as the preferred mating choice. The purest and most satisfying form of this competition is the sport of MMA, man-to-man combat. No racquets, no end zones, no infield fly rule—just two men of the same size, physically and mentally prepared to the utmost, locked inside a cage attacking each other with minimal rules.

I don't care for most sports. I just find them boring. The excitement generally is manufactured like a "championship" game. There's just not that much excitement for me in watching a group of guys trying to hit a ball with a stick, and even with the prize of a "world championship" up for grabs, I still can't get into it.

Sure, they're mostly harmless and even beneficial to their participants. All sports are disciplines, and like any discipline, they can provide you with an increased understanding of yourself and the confidence boost that comes with the experience of accomplishing a difficult task, but really all sports are just watered down fighting.

They use a ball and helmets and goals, but in actual truth—they just want to fight. The ball, the rules, all of that was invented because someone wanted to compete, but they didn't want the humiliation that comes from getting your ass kicked. The reason why some men show aggression even in defeat in many sports is that deep down they are in denial that they have been conquered.

When a guy slam dunks a basketball in your face and then taunts you, "You like that, bitch?" what he's trying to say is that he just beat your ass. He just owned you in the agreed on competition. It's hard to swallow and the "owned" man will almost always talk shit back. He doesn't feel "dominated." He might feel frustrated that he can't stop the superior player, but he doesn't feel like he has had his ass kicked. Oftentimes he will take comfort in the belief that while this guy can beat him in basketball, if he could grab this guy outside, he would shut him up. See, that's the difference between fighting and other sports—when you get your ass kicked in a fight, you can't say, "Yeah, well I can dunk a basketball on him," because no one cares. Beating someone's ass is the definitive end point of all sports.

What the UFC and the sport of MMA represent is the most dynamic form of human competition possible, and once you get involved in it, it's very difficult to get excited about watching someone trying to hit a ball with a stick.

Warriors of the Ultimate Fighting™ Championship®

Introduction

In a sandy fighting pit, thousands of years ago in ancient Greece, two hand-to-hand combatants covered in dust, sweat, and blood clashed together under the blaze of the sun. With an hour of back-and-forth battle already behind them, both athletes suffered from painful wounds, dehydration, and fatigue, but neither of them would submit. They continued to throw their fists and feet with bone-shattering conviction. They continued to take their opponent to the ground, where they struggled to apply strangleholds and joint locks. Both fighters had worked a lifetime to earn the right to compete in the games in ancient Olympia. And now that they were here, watched by thousands of spectators from three nations, they welcomed death before defeat.

All fighters, having abandoned the luxuries of normal men to follow the path of the combative athlete, came prepared to endure the pain and duration of battle. In local gymnasiums, they'd developed the strength and stamina to compete in a sport without weight classes or time limits by climbing miles of rope and lifting heavy barrels. Under the guidance of former champions, they had mastered the arts of boxing and wrestling, both of which were mandatory for surviving a contest that permitted all holds and strikes, save for biting and gouging. Only after

years of enduring punishment that turned their faces into leather, their knuckles into stone, and their ears into disfigured cauliflower-like lumps were they allowed to test their skills outside of training in actual pankration (combining wrestling with boxing) tournaments, the most respected sport in all of ancient Greece.

Victories at local athletic festivals earned the fighters prize money to pay for their trainers and expensive diet of meat. Triumphs at national tournaments, held throughout the Mediterranean, brought them fame and honor comparable to that of the greatest soldiers on the battlefield. But it was the games in Olympia, also known as the Sacred Crown Games, that all pankratiasts strived to reach. There they could test their skills against the strongest, most skilled combative athletes on earth. There, on a dusty patch of earth, they could stamp their name in history.

Although the last man standing in the Olympic pankration tournament received only an olive-leaf wreath for his accomplishment, when he returned home, his community pampered him like a king. Merchants refused to accept his money, statues were erected in his honor, and pottery depicting his hulking physique was mass-produced and sold in the market. But such rewards were considered trivial when compared to the rewards

1

offered by the gods. Despite being born into this world like all men, the pankratiasts crowned at the Olympic Games were bestowed the gift of everlasting life. Long after their bodies perished, their spirit, strength, and courage would remain on earth for others to admire. With the heroic deeds of the lone soldier having been lost among expanding armies and massive battlefields, the Olympics gave birth to a new kind of hero.

On the night of November 12, 1993, centuries after the Greek Olympics were abolished by the conquering Roman Empire, fight fans packed into McNichols Arena in Denver, Colorado, to witness eight martial artists from a variety of disciplines such as karate, sumo, submission fighting, and jujitsu square off in a full-contact elimination tournament to declare an ultimate champion. Just as in pankration, no time limits or weight classes, and the only rules were no biting or gouging. In an octagon-shaped ring surrounded by a chain link fence called the Octagon, combatants headed into battle to test their courage, their stamina, and their fighting techniques.

Spectators witnessed a downed man get his head repeatedly stomped. They watched a four-hundred-pound sumo wrestler be kicked square in the mouth, sending a tooth flying from the cage. It was unlike any competition the spectators had ever seen, but what truly stunned the thousands in attendance, and the hundreds of thousands watching on pay-per-view around the world, was how a lanky, 178-pound jiu-jitsu practitioner from Brazil won the title belt by taking his opponents to the mat, wrapping his body around them like a snake, and then forcing them to submit under the agonizing pressure of a chokehold. Royce Gracie, the smallest man in the tournament, had bested some of the world's toughest

hand-to-hand combatants without throwing a single worthy punch.

It was a dream that came true for Rorion Gracie, Royce's older brother. He had come to the United States from Brazil almost twenty years before to teach his family's style of jiu-jitsu, but with the West infatuated with Bruce Lee movies and whirling kicks, no one had given ground fighting a chance. For years he had toiled to find a way to make people understand what he was trying to teach. Rorion had showed videotapes of his family fighting in Brazil to anyone who cared to watch. He had defeated dozens of kickboxers and karate black belts in challenge matches held in the garage of his home in Hermosa Beach, California. Whatever he could think of to help spread the word about Gracie Jiu-Jitsu had been done, and still his family's fighting art had remained in obscurity.

Then Rorion came up with the idea of the Ultimate Fighting Championship (UFC). He brought in people in the entertainment industry who met with the cable companies and recruited experienced fighters from around the world. He planned everything down to the last detail, making sure that there were no rules or restrictions that could lead competitors to claim that their fighting styles only worked in true street fights. Everything had to be perfect because this was his chance to prove, once and for all, the importance of learning how to fight on the ground. "It was amazing to see how surprised those guys were," said Rorion. "Royce got them in the clinch and they had no idea what the heck happened. They must have thought someone pulled the carpet from underneath them. For them it was a shock, but for my family and me it was just another day at the office."

The majority of spectators didn't fully understand how Royce dispensed with his opponents so quickly on the ground, and whether they admired him or loathed him, his skill intrigued them. They wanted to learn about his style of fighting and to see how it would compare with other martial arts styles that hadn't been in the first show, and as a result, the event became more than a one-time extravaganza.

The UFC became one of the fastest growing pay-per-view events of all time, and each event became a learning experience for the entire martial arts world. Champions such as Royce Gracie were cast into the international spotlight, and the courage and heart that fighters displayed in the Octagon encouraged others to dedicate their lives to the new combative challenge. With only a dream and desire, future competitors began to train up to eight hours a day, strengthening their bodies, sharpening their skills, hardening their minds, and developing their own individualistic fighting styles.

For many beginners, their first challenges came in local UFC-style tournaments that had popped up in gymnasiums and American Indian Casinos around the country. After building up their skills, reputation, and ability to endure pain, a handful of combatants found themselves traveling to events that had emerged overseas, entertaining thousands with their devastating strikes and stealthy ground skills. Just as pankratiasts had struggled to reach the games in ancient Olympia, now modern combatants strove to reach the UFC, an event that continued to bring together the strongest and most technical fighters in the world. At each show, a more knowledgeable group of combatants entered the competition in an attempt to dethrone the reigning champions of the Octagon. Brazilian Jiu-Jitsu was put to the test against a host of amateur

wrestlers who had spent their whole life battling an opponent on the ground, as well as a number of strikers who had learned how to defend themselves against submissions. With athletes who were better versed in all aspects of the fighting game, the quick knockouts and submissions became harder to come by, leading to exciting and technical matches that more closely resembled the tournaments in ancient Greece.

The UFC was traveling down the path to becoming a legitimate sporting event, but along the way it encountered a devastating blockade. The early events had been sensationalized as a blood sport to garner appeal. The promoters who had taken the show over from the Gracie family did everything they could to shed this image, but the stereotype remained, especially with the general population who had not kept up with the continuous evolution of the sport. The debate of whether no holds barred tournaments should be made illegal was ignited and hit the newspapers and talk shows with an evangelic fervor. UFC fans went to great lengths to defend the brave warriors who stepped into the Octagon, but with the opposition being backed by the boxing world and its constituents, both of whom felt threatened by the UFC's rising popularity, the debate eventually reached the courtroom, and the groundbreaking event found itself on the losing side of the battle. Banned in many states, politicians such as Senator John McCain from Arizona began referring to the event as "human cock fighting." A negative stigma clung to all those involved in the sport, and as a result, UFC 12, held on February 8, 1997, was the last event to be carried by the major cable providers.

Although the event survived underground (through websites and word-of-mouth), the UFC had been robbed of its main source of revenue.

Fighter purses dwindled, and with the UFC being out of the public eye, the crowds at the events began to grow thin. It could have been the death of the newly emerging sport, burying it for another two thousand years, but fortunately it wasn't about money or fame for the majority of the fighters. They began the sport to answer a simple question—what martial arts style is the most effective? Through twelve UFC tournaments, filled with almost a hundred grueling matches, they had received their answer: no one style was the best. "Back in the beginning, everyone competing in the UFC had a lot of respect for other competitors who had a similar martial arts background," said Mark Coleman, a true legend of the Octagon. "Wrestlers stuck with other wrestlers. Strikers stuck with other strikers, and the jiu-jitsu guys stuck with other grapplers. But then things began to evolve so much that if you were just a wrestler, just a striker, or just a grappler, then you were in a lot of trouble. That's when it became mixed martial arts (MMA). Everyone started getting along, and we all tried to take the sport to the next level."

In this new age, combatants no longer considered themselves karate practitioners or jiu-jitsu stylists; they considered themselves MMA fighters. Combining the grueling training regimens of both professional boxers and amateur wrestlers, UFC competitors became some of the best-conditioned athletes in sports. With their matches offering amazing displays of sportsmanship, courage, and technique, widespread interest in the sport began to resurface despite the cable ban. Now all the UFC needed was to get sanctioning from the various states.

In July 1999, the UFC invited Lorenzo Fertitta, a Las Vegas, Nevada, business executive and vice chairperson of the Nevada State Athletic

Commission, to attend their twenty-first event in Cedar Rapids, Iowa. Lorenzo saw the fighters' tremendous athletic ability, but coming from a boxing background, he didn't equate striking a downed opponent with sportsmanship. Shortly thereafter, he resigned from the commission to become president of Station Casinos, a publicly held gaming company founded by his family. On the side, Lorenzo and his longtime friend, fight promoter Dana White, decided to begin a boxing promotion. The idea also drew the interest of Lorenzo's older brother, Frank Fertitta III, chairperson and chief executive of Station Casinos. While exploring the details, Lorenzo and White ran into UFC competitors Kimo and John Lewis one evening at the Hard Rock Hotel in Las Vegas. A huge fan of all fighting arts, White decided to personally experience the art of ground fighting and began taking private jiu-jitsu lessons from Lewis. White liked it so well, in fact, that he convinced Lorenzo and then Frank to do the same. Within weeks, all three fell in love with the sport and began to follow the action in the UFC.

Then White went a step further and started managing the careers of two fast-rising UFC fighters, Tito Ortiz and Chuck Liddell. While negotiating an Ortiz contract, he learned that UFC founder Bob Meyrowitz was looking for a partner. White immediately called the Fertittas. They felt the market was right to move the UFC into mainstream sports, and agreed it would take more than money. They would have to educate athletic commissioners, political leaders, cable television executives and even loyal fans, many of whom still favored fights between traditional karate practitioners. Money was necessary, but the only way for the UFC to grow was for it to be recognized as a legitimate sport. The Fertittas knew that with their financial resources and

White's business expertise they could achieve that goal. Instead of becoming a partner, they formed a sports entertainment company, Zuffa, LLC, and purchased the UFC outright.

In January 2001, White became president of the UFC. He and the Fertittas first approached the California Athletic Commission, the New Jersey State Athletic Control Board, and the Nevada State Athletic Commission, and these organizations listened to what the two promoters had to say. They brought fighters to meetings with cable company executives. They worked with the athletic commissions to adopt new rules that included weight classes and banned techniques such as kicking a downed opponent in the head. They introduced a new marketing campaign that put the UFC on consumer television and radio and in national magazines such as Maxim and Sports Illustrated. Most importantly, they hired a great team that could lead the charge into the next phase of the Ultimate Fighting Championship. In a matter of months, the Zuffa team accomplished more than the previous UFC owners had in six years. They recruited a stable of world-class athletes, had the sport sanctioned in New Jersey and Nevada, and convinced the major cable operators to carry again the event on live pay-per-view.

On February 23, 2001, the new UFC brand was reintroduced at the Trump Taj Mahal in Atlantic City, New Jersey. Fight fans did not see traditional karate practitioners matched against experienced grapplers. They didn't see one-sided beatings or quick tap outs. Instead they saw wrestlers who could punch and kick and strikers who could flawlessly execute a submission hold. It was no longer a comparison of styles, but a comparison of individuals. The victors were those who possessed strength, stamina, and knowledge of fighting while standing and on the ground. It did not take long for fans to realize that it was no longer a spectacle, but a legitimate sport.

Today, much like the ancient Greek Olympics, the UFC has given birth to a new kind of hero, one who is measured more by the size of his heart and courage than his fighting style. Every fighter understands that he has to be proficient in grappling, wrestling, and striking in order to be effective in the Octagon, but each fighter has a primary focus. The wrestlers, fearful of a strikers' punches and kicks, practice takedowns for hours on end, adjusting the angles of their attack so they can swoop in on an opponent and slam him to the ground. The submission fighters, no longer armed with a bag of foreign tricks, learn new ways to catch their prey and choke them unconscious. And the strikers, fearful of getting taken to the ground, improve upon their footwork, firing jabs and crosses as they dance across the ring. With the competition getting fiercer at each event, and the athletes hungrier for the title belt, UFC champions work past their mental and physical limits to hold onto glory.

Now, for the first time, the most dedicated warriors on the planet divulge the secrets to their success. For some it is agonizing training regimens and grueling diets, and for others it is battling their own demons to find courage. Celebrated MMA champions such as Pedro Rizzo, Ken Shamrock, and BJ Penn, men whose names have been added to the list of warriors to be remembered, bring you down their long path, through the adrenaline rush and the pain of defeat, to reach the top of the MMA mountain.

SECTION ONE

The Submission Fighters

Ground Rules

With blood still glistening on the canvas from the night's previous bouts, Gerard Gordeau, a ruthless kickboxer from Amsterdam, stepped into the Octagon on November 12, 1993, at UFC1, to wage the final battle for the UFC's first title belt. In his quarterfinal bout, he had bested 410-pound sumo wrestler Teila Tuli in a matter of seconds with a roundhouse kick to the mouth and thunderous right hand to the temple. In the semifinals, he had battered fellow kickboxer Kevin Rosier to the canvas with a barrage of leg kicks and jabs and then finished him off with a foot stomp to the liver. Gordeau had given the crowd the two most dramatic finishes of the evening, but they had come at a price. His knockout hand was badly broken and beginning to swell, and he had two of Teila Tuli's teeth embedded in the top of his right foot.

Despite his injuries, Gordeau confidently stared down his opponent, Royce Gracie. The 178-pound jiu-jitsu practitioner looked as fresh as when the night of battle had begun. He'd avoided receiving even a single punch by taking both of his previous fights to the ground, a tactic few of the competitors had anticipated. Gordeau wouldn't let that happen. He had been fighting his entire life on the street and in the ring. He knew how to knock out an opponent, especially one who had virtually no defenses on his feet. Once Gracie got close, Gordeau would lay into him with a punch or a kick or a knee. This time when the grappler went to the canvas, he would be sleeping.

But the match didn't go according to his game plan. Shortly after the referee slashed his hand through the air, signaling the beginning of the match, Gordeau found himself lying on his back with Gracie riding his weight on top of him. Everything had happened so fast. Gracie had ducked low and shot in, giving Gordeau no room to strike. Gordeau had tried to push him away, fight him off, and then one of his legs was yanked out from underneath him. He wasn't quite sure how he had gone down, but he knew this was not where he wanted to be. Gordeau looked up into his opponent's determined eyes, and knew that his survival obviously depended on getting back to his feet. Instinctively, he rolled over onto his stomach and attempted to labor up with his opponent attached to his back. But before Gordeau made it to his knees, a panicky feeling stole through him as he felt an arm slither around his neck. His air was cut off and then the blood to his brain. His world began to fade, grow black. Warmth washing through his body, he understood that he was at Gracie's mercy, and he tapped in submission.

As Royce Gracie received the title belt of the first UFC, his older brother Rorion Gracie watched proudly from the sidelines. Rorion had struggled for nearly twenty years to introduce the art of Gracie Jiu-Jitsu to the world, and now, after almost a year organizing the first UFC, he had finally realized his dream. No one could claim that Royce had gotten lucky because he had defeated three competitors in a single night. No one could claim that he had won based on size because he was the smallest competitor in the event. Rorion could have easily used one of his other brothers, several of whom were more accomplished fighters, but he had chosen Royce to be the family representative in the show because he knew that it would be a very convincing example of what jiu-jitsu could do for people.

"You look at Royce, you almost feel sorry for him," said Rorion. "He is a little string bean. You see a little guy beat a big guy, it is proof of how effective this stuff is."

Almost overnight Royce created an entirely new mystique that surrounded anyone who knew how to fight on the ground. Word began to spread that if someone studied Gracie Jiu-Jitsu for just a few months, that person could defeat a black belt in karate or kung fu. When a karate stylist boasted that he could break ten boards with a single punch, people shot back with, "Yeah, but do you know how to grapple?" When watercooler conversations arose about who was the toughest fighter on the planet, the name Royce Gracie was inevitably thrown into the pile with Bruce Lee and Chuck Norris.

In his first match in the Octagon, Royce Gracie takes professional boxer Art Jimmerson to the canvas, then climbs into the mount. Just as Gracie prepares to attack, Jimmerson taps in submission. The entire bout lasts just over two minutes.

Royce Gracie mounts fifty-two-year-old karate practitioner Ron Van Clief before putting him away with a choke in under four minutes.

Schools across the country that taught traditional styles were in an uproar. They wanted to show the world that what they had to offer wasn't a scam or a hoax and that they hadn't pulled the wool over everyone's eyes for the past thousand years. So in the second event, hundreds of traditional martial artists sent applications into the UFC hoping to avenge their styles against Gracie Jiu-Jitsu. But once again the karate and kung-fu practitioners who secured a slot in the event failed to land an effective blow on the fighter from Brazil. While many quickly scrambled for excuses as to why Royce had been so dominant yet again, others sucked up their pride and sought to relearn the fighting arts.

Royce continued to demonstrate the superiority of ground fighting as he fought his way through the competition. In UFC 4, he choked out karate legend Ron Van Clief in his quarterfinal match, secured an arm bar in the semifinals on karate practitioner Keith Hackney (who had bested a 620-pound sumo wrestler in the previous event), and then took home yet another title belt after defeating world-renowned amateur wrestler Dan Severn in the finals. "Royce made one message very clear—if you do not know how to fight on the ground, then you will be lost," said Rorion. "That was the message, and people understood what they had to do. I had to keep expanding my school until I ended up with a 14,000-square-foot training facility. It is the biggest jiu-jitsu school in the world. I began teaching so many people. I could have just held onto all that knowledge so that my family would keep winning for the next seventy years, just as we had for the past seventy years in Brazil. But

Hermes Franca nails Richard Crunkilton with a hard right cross.

Bringing the fight to the ground, Hermes Franca works to secure a triangle choke on Richard Crunkilton.

Richard Crunkilton makes a desperate escape.

Hermes Franca dislocates Richard Crunkilton's elbow. Amazingly, Crunkilton continues to fight.

With his legs tightening like a vice, Genki Sudo attempts to secure a triangle choke on Leigh Remedios.

After UFC 5, held on April 7, 1995, Royce chose to bow out of the UFC with his nearly flawless record intact, but the impact he had made on the martial arts would last forever. "Everyone started learning jiu-jitsu, and now there is pretty much a level playing field," said Rorion. "When you see no holds barred fighting today, what determines the winner is no longer the best martial arts style, because everyone does jiu-jitsu. Everyone knows a little bit of grappling. I saw this coming from a mile away, but as I have already said, I have never regretted it. Gracie Jiu-Jitsu has changed the martial arts for the better, forever."

Clinging to Leigh Remedios, Genki Sudo lands a strike.

that was not ethically right. Jiu-jitsu is something so beneficial to humankind in general that I could not have kept it for myself out of selfishness. So I put the knowledge out there to help the world, and I have never regretted it. Some of the most rewarding moments are when I receive letters from so-called 'weaklings' who studied Gracie Jiu-Jitsu from my instructional videotapes, and then used that knowledge to defend themselves in actual street fights."

With the fighting secrets of the Gracie family being studied by thousands, it was only a matter of time before competitors began to catch up.

Murilo Bustamante attempts an arm bar on Matt Lindland.

Frank Mir works to secure the arm of Wes Sims.

The Prodigy

In the new and improved UFC, it had grown increasingly more difficult for even the most accomplished jiu-jitsu stylists to pull out a victory on grappling technique alone. BJ Penn realized this shortly after he stepped into the Octagon in UFC 32, held on June 29, 2001, to face Din Thomas, one of the most respected strikers in the newly revamped lightweight division.

Penn was hoping to end the fight with a submission and shot in for the takedown, but Thomas managed to keep the fight standing by countering with a sprawl. In retaliation, Penn tied up in the clinch and performed a classic Gracie move by pulling Thomas down between his legs, into his guard, where he quickly secured an arm bar. In the past, this most likely would have been the end of the line for a striker, but Thomas knew exactly how to power out of the hold. When Penn stood back up, Thomas stepped forward and targeted his head with a powerful right hook.

Instead of Penn shooting his body underneath the punch as most grapplers had been trained to do, he abandoned his original game plan and avoided the hit like a boxer. Then, with his opponent overextended, he cupped the back of Thomas's head and brought up a thunderous knee to the jaw. If that wasn't enough to surprise the spectators in attendance, Penn followed his unconscious victim to the floor and finished him off with three devastating punches. As it turned out, BJ Penn was one of the most impressive strikers in the lightweight division, showing just how much jiu-jitsu stylists had evolved since the days of Royce Gracie. The distinction between a grappler and a striker had become a very fine line.

Growing up in Hilo, Hawaii, BJ Penn spent the majority of his adolescence hanging out at the beach with his friends and fighting on the streets. Having reigned victorious in over seventy fistfights by his seventeenth birthday, Penn began to think he was the toughest scrapper on the Island. Then a tae kwon do instructor by the name of Tom Callis came to his front door in search of sparring partners. "My friends and me were always into boxing, and we would all go to my backyard after school and take turns boxing each other all the way into the night,"

BJ Penn knocking Din Thomas out with a solid knee to the jaw.

said Penn. "That tae kwon do instructor moved in six or seven houses down the road from me and saw what we were doing, and he wanted me to wrestle with him because he had taken a couple of jiu-jitsu classes from Ralph Gracie out in California. I told him, 'Screw that, let's spar!' I thought I was the toughest guy in the world, and that it would be a waste of my time. But the guy kept coming to my house, and eventually my father made me go train with him so he would stop coming over. When we got onto the mats, he tapped me out with an arm bar."

Thinking Callis had only gotten lucky, Penn went after him again and again, but each time he found himself tapping in submission. In the course of just a few hours, Penn realized that he knew absolutely nothing about fighting. Instead of growing frustrated, he put his ego aside and returned the very next day prepared to learn.

Over the next few months, Penn discovered

that he had the same natural talent for grappling as he did for punching. He learned how to choke an opponent out, bend an arm to the point of breaking, and defend himself while lying on his back. "It got to the point where I could tap Tom out pretty easily," said Penn. "He was heading to California to test for his black belt in tae kwon do, and he asked me if I wanted to go with him because we would be real close to Ralph Gracie's school. I thought I was pretty good, and I went along thinking I would tap out everyone. I really didn't know anything, and so everyone at the school beat me. But I guess I did pretty well for it being my first time because Ralph Gracie told Tom that I had a future in the sport. When we got back, Tom told my dad. At the time, I wasn't doing anything back home. I was just hanging out at the beach, partying, and getting into trouble with my friends. My dad wanted me off the

island, but I didn't want to go. He eventually said that in six months he was going to send me to the mainland to check out the school and train. To make him happy I agreed, thinking that the day would never come. But when that day did come, I almost wanted to cry. He forced me to go, and so I came to the mainland to train."

Moving to California changed everything. Penn hadn't any friends to hang out with, or friends to go out looking for trouble with, so he devoted all his time to training, sometimes going to the gym as often as three times a day. In a matter of weeks, he passed the other white belts in class, and within months he could put up a struggle against even the most advanced students. In all of Ralph Gracie's years teaching jiu-jitsu, he had never seen anything like it. The boy was a true prodigy. "For me, everything was fighting oriented," said Penn. "My friend showed

Mounted on top of Joey Gilbert, BJ Penn fires away with punches.

BJ Penn lands a left hook that knocks Caol Uno out cold.

BJ Penn follows an unconscious Caol Uno to the ground and finishes him off with punches.

me a tape of jiu-jitsu competition, and I really didn't care much for it. I wasn't interested in sport jiu-jitsu; I wasn't even happy to be there. Then a white belt competition came up, and my instructor wanted me to compete in it. He said I would crush all the guys, because I could beat all the other white belts at the school. So I went down, and I beat everyone in my weight and in the open division. After that, when I was still a white belt, I went to Joe Moreira's Blue Belt International and submitted everyone there in the blue belt division. From there I started liking the feeling of competition and understanding what it was about."

As one tournament led to another, Penn finally found some direction in his life. Always looking forward to the next competition and constantly striving to get better, he was missing the late-night parties less and less. He soon realized that scrapping on the street wasn't all that he had believed it to be. Although Hilo would always be his home, he started to feel all right about not being there. He needed this break to find his bearings, and he made the most out of his time away from those he loved. He poured his heart and soul into training, and then, just three and a half years after he had come to the mainland, he received his black belt in jiu-jitsu. Such a feat was

BJ Penn lands a high kick on Jens Pulver.

BJ Penn works to bring Jens Pulver to the ground.

Mounted on top of Jens Pulver, BJ Penn fires downward punches.

Jens Pulver tags
BJ Penn with his
famous left hook.

BJ Penn suffers his first loss in the UFC to Jens Pulver.

almost unheard of. Most students trained for eight years before they were even considered for black belt.

If anyone had any qualms as to whether one deserved such an honor so early in his training, Penn changed their minds when he traveled to Brazil to compete. Climbing onto the mats with some of the most feared and respected jiu-jitsu practitioners in the world, his victories continued to accumulate. By the time he boarded the plane to head back to California, he had become the first non-Brazilian to win the Jiu-Jitsu World Championships. "I didn't really realize what I had accomplished at the time," said Penn. "But now, as time goes by, I look back more often, and it is beginning to sink in."

Although Penn had dominated at the top levels of sport jiu-jitsu and had gone about as far as he could go, he didn't hang up his gi (uniform) and head back home to Hawaii. Still only twenty years old, he felt there was more to accomplish, and he set his sights on the mixed martial arts (MMA) competition. He had seen enough UFC events, however, to realize that jiu-jitsu technique alone was not enough to dominate in the Octagon. "One of the first things I had to work on was wrestling," said Penn. "It is not a fighting sport, but you can definitely use wrestling in a fight. It is just as technical on the takedown aspect as jiu-jitsu is on submissions and ground work. In jiu-jitsu, I never learned any takedowns. All they ever did was show me the ground. So I started wrestling all the time to improve on my takedowns, and now I consider my style more of a blend between jiu-jitsu and wrestling. I think the two combined is the ultimate grappling art."

To learn how to put his wrestling, jiu-jitsu, and striking together in a fight, Penn branched out and trained with new partners, including UFC veteran John Lewis, who was heavily connected

with the MMA world. Before long, Penn found himself rolling around on the mats with Dana White, the president of the UFC. "They knew that I could grapple, but they didn't know if I would make a good fighter," said Penn. "Nobody knew that I'd been fighting all my life. They all thought of me as a jiu-jitsu guy."

White was hesitant about bringing the young grappler into the show simply because Penn had never before competed in a match in which his opponent could strike. The UFC had evolved since the days of Royce Gracie, and a competitor couldn't survive in the Octagon on submissions alone. But after rolling around with Penn on the mat, falling victim to his lightning-fast submissions, White decided to give him a chance in UFC 31: *Locked and Loaded*, on May 4, 2001, at the Trump Taj Mahal in Atlantic City, New Jersey.

On the night of the big show, Penn stood in the locker room backstage and gazed at his reflection in the mirror. This was the moment he had been waiting for since he first left Hawaii— the chance to prove to his father and to himself that all those years scrapping on the street could still be channeled in a positive direction. "Looking into the mirror, I stepped out of myself," said Penn. "I knew it was going to be different than a jiu-jitsu tournament. In jiu-jitsu you can win with skill. In a fight, you have to win with your heart and mind. I had seen other fighters win based on skill, and they get too comfortable; it sets them up for a downfall. The guy with fire in his eyes is going to kick everyone's ass. The only way to fight is out of fire—just come out with guns blazing. Usually I'm a quiet, timid person, but before I fight, I separate myself. Nothing goes through my head except winning."

When Penn heard his name called, he turned away from his reflection, climbed a set of stairs, and began his journey past the aisles of reaching

BJ Penn struggles to submit Caol Uno in their rematch. "I was going to try to put him down, mount him, punch him, and if he gave his back, then I would go for the choke," says Penn. "But that was the thing, I didn't even try to choke him once. I didn't do anything."

fans. His previous accomplishments gave him instant prestige, but the reputation of Brazilian Jiu-Jitsu no longer carried the weight that it once had. In order to capture the hearts of the fans, Penn would have to prove himself.

In the opening seconds of the bout, Penn advanced on his opponent, Joey Gilbert, with a flurry of strikes. "My game plan was to handle the match like a typical street fight," said Penn. "I was going to punch him in the face, put him on his back, and then beat him up on the ground." Everything went just as he had anticipated, and after five minutes lashing out with strikes and scrambling on the ground, Penn had his opponent right where he wanted him—belly down on the canvas. Riding his weight on top of his opponent, Penn unleashed the demon inside of him

and began unloading a serious of hammering fists into the sides of Gilbert's head, forcing a referee stoppage.

It wasn't until Penn untangled himself from his opponent, stood up, and heard the theme song of the UFC echo throughout the arena that he realized what he had just achieved. He had won his first bout in the UFC by way of knockout. It was the perfect debut because he not only got to show his jiu-jitsu skills by taking a dominant position on the ground, but he also got to show that he could strike with the best of them. "It was the most important fight of my life," said Penn. "No fight will ever compare to that one, because it was like I had lost my virginity. I can't describe the feeling I had standing in the Octagon, listening to the music of the UFC. I felt

Caol Uno clings to BJ Penn's arms to avoid a chokehold.

goose bumps and chills all over my body. I realized that I was finally where I needed to be." There would be no stopping Penn; he had begun his reign of terror in the Octagon.

After defeating Thomas in the next event with a solid knee to the face, Penn climbed another rung of the ladder when he entered UFC 34: *High Voltage*, on November 2, 2001, at the MGM Grand Hotel in Las Vegas, Nevada, to battle Caol Uno, a world-renowned submission tactician from Japan. Although many people thought the match would be an amazing display of grappling techniques, Penn ended the fight with a lightning-fast barrage of punches to his opponent's face. The entire bout lasted eleven seconds.

Leaving his first three opponents lying devastated on the canvas, Penn became one of the

most popular fighters in MMA competition. He had all the makings of a champion, so in UFC 35: *Throwdown*, held on January 11, 2002, at the Mohegan Sun Casino, in Uncasville, Connecticut, after only three MMA fights, promoters gave him a shot to steal the title belt from reigning lightweight champion Jens Pulver, a strong wrestler who could punch like a professional boxer. Penn did not take this fight lightly. Many other top MMA lightweights had entered the Octagon to take the title belt, but Pulver had beaten them back one by one.

In the months leading up to the fight, Penn began to feel the pressure. Everyone expected him to win, including the odds makers in the various Las Vegas casinos. They thought he could take Pulver on the ground as well as on his feet and that he would destroy the current champion in the first round. There was so much hype surrounding their match, in fact, that UFC promoters decided to make it the first lightweight bout in history to be the main event. Everywhere Penn went, people smiled at him and clapped him on the back, as if he had already won.

Despite his nerves having worn him down both mentally and physically, Penn entered the Octagon on the night of November 2, 2001, fully believing he would be victorious. When Pulver came at him in the opening seconds of the bout, firing with punches, Penn ducked a fist headed directly towards his face and then simultaneously drove his shoulders into Pulver's hips and seized his legs. When they hit the canvas, Penn came out on top. Immediately, he began searching for a limb that he could twist or bend. But Pulver did everything right. He kept his arms in and his head straight. "Back in the old days when Royce Gracie brought a karate guy to the mat, he could get a submission almost at will," said Penn. "Now UFC competitors never let that happen, especially their champions. You can barely get your arms up on his ribs, he's blocking your legs down, and he's punching you. It's a whole lot harder to put your opponent in pain than it used to be."

Penn knew, however, that the longer he kept the fight on the ground, the greater his chances were of getting a submission. So when Pulver managed to shove him away with his feet and stand back up, Penn leapt on him. They collided with force, but somehow Pulver managed to keep his footing. Instead of sliding off, Penn wrapped both his legs around Pulver's waist and his right arm around his head. With Pulver staggering across the Octagon, carrying both of their weights, Penn clinched his right arm tight, trying

to sink his forearm deep into Pulver's throat. "If you get them in a choke, they're gone," said Penn. "It's the deadliest submission there is. A couple of years ago in practice, I was going for this move where I always got caught in a choke. I kept doing it and doing it, and every time I got choked. Then one time I managed to get that move without getting choked, and I thought that I was the man. A few seconds later, I woke up with piss all over myself, and I realized I didn't escape after all. I had just passed out."

Penn was hoping to put his opponent in the same predicament, but Pulver remained calm, placed a hand on Penn's elbow, and then slowly peeled the constricting arm up over his face. As the first round progressed, Penn had to work harder and harder to get the takedown. "You have to have some balls," said Penn. "If you are fighting an experienced striker with some wrestling ability, you can't just move around and set up a takedown. You have to get into an exchange, because that is the only way to catch him off guard. If you stay on the outside and never go to punch at him, he is just teeing off, and you're trying to shoot and he is sprawling. It is never going to work. If you stay on the outside, you're going to get knocked out anyway. You might as well go in and try to punch him with all your might. As soon as you get into that exchange, then you go for the takedown."

Penn let his hands fly, and although he managed to take Pulver repeatedly to the ground in the remainder of the first round and the beginning of the second, his opponent kept fending off his submissions and finding his way back to his feet. It wasn't until two minutes remained in the second round that Penn's determination paid off. After taking a tiring Pulver to the ground again, he managed to climb into the mount position,

BJ Penn lands a front kick to Caol Uno. "I fought just on skills," says Penn. "I didn't put any heart into it; I didn't fight like a champion. That is why it ended in a draw."

seize his opponent's wrist, and then swing around to the side for an arm bar. Pulver clamped his hands together, a last ditch effort to save himself, but Penn continued to apply pressure. Just as Penn broke the arm free and extended it, the buzzer sounded and the referee pulled them apart.

Because Penn had been robbed of the victory, he lost focus when he came out for the third round. He continued to try to take Pulver to the mat, but his shots were not as sharp or quick, and Pulver managed to fend most of them off by

sprawling. The bout turned into a stand-up war, one in which Pulver got the upper hand.

When the fight fell into the hands of the judges after five grueling rounds, Pulver received a unanimous decision. It was the first loss of Penn's career. "I choked," said Penn. "I couldn't take the pressure. You know what they say, 'Don't do something great if you can't take the congratulations.' I just wasn't ready at the time. I wasn't mature enough to be a champion. To be a champion, you have to have losses. You have to have draws. You have to know what it feels like to be beat up. You have to know what it feels like when you and your opponent come to a standstill and you are just hitting each other back and forth. You have to go through all those emotions to be a complete fighter. I needed all that good stuff."

While he understood that every fighter needs to feel the sting of defeat, it didn't take away any of the pain. Penn tried jumping right back into training, but he no longer had the drive that had carried him so far. Failing to find a way to lift the depression, he eventually decided to move back home to Hilo.

Spending time with his family and friends did wonders to lift his spirits. His greatest fear about coming back was that he would revert to his old ways, but shortly after he arrived, he knew that could never happen. Jiu-jitsu and MMA competition had given him direction in life, and while he still barbecued with his friends on Sunday, sharing the occasional beer, he knew his desire to compete would keep him on the straight and narrow.

After Penn had settled in, he resumed training with a new intensity and outlook. In the past he had allowed all his various coaches to dictate his training, but with each one pulling him in a different direction, he had lost his focus on his primary game plan—winning the fight. "So I told myself that from now on I would only listen to myself while training for a fight," said Penn. "During the off season I'll do whatever my trainers think is right, but when I train for a fight, I'll be the one calling the shots. I'll say what I am doing today. I'll say what punches I should throw, because I'm going to be the one in there fighting. I'll train too hard on purpose, and I will have other guys on the side who will tell me when to stop. If I'm tired of my routine and want

to do something new, I'll grab some goggles, go out to the ocean, and then pick up a hundred-pound rock from under the water and see how far I can carry it. If I want to do something new, really push myself, sometimes I will go up to a high waterfall and jump off, even though I'm scared to death. Even five days before a fight, right before I need to go to the UFC, I'm still taking chances like that, chances where I could get hurt. I need to keep the edge all the time."

Although Penn suffered a disappointing draw with Uno during their rematch in UFC 41, he used that edge against Matt Hughes in UFC 46: *Supernatural*, on January 31, 2004, at the Mandalay Bay Events Center in Las Vegas. Penn, going to the next weight division, stepped into the Octagon with a wrestler known for slamming his victims to the canvas and then dismantling them with strikes. Penn, however, used his superlative strikes and submission skills to dominate from the onset, and then he finished off his feared opponent with a rear naked choke toward the end of the first round, leading to one of the most impressive upsets in UFC history.

Everyday Penn thanks the people who made it possible for him to have achieved his childhood dream of becoming one of the best fighters ever to walk the earth. "If it wasn't for Royce Gracie and his family, I wouldn't be here right now," said Penn. "I would still be drinking and partying with my friends, thinking I was the toughest guy in the world. They flipped the whole world upside down. They made me believe in what they had to give. If God said to me that I could only study one style for the rest of my life, it would have to be jiu-jitsu—I wouldn't pick anything else. It has just given me so much, I can't even describe it."

The World's Most Dangerous Man

With almost fifteen thousand fight fans packed into the auditorium of Las Vegas, Nevada's, MGM Grand Hotel/Casino and millions more watching at home on pay-per-view around the world, on November 22, 2002, Ken Shamrock, the first ever UFC Superfight champion and one of the most popular fighters in all of mixed martial arts (MMA) competition, emerged from a billow of smoke and lights and began his descent toward the Octagon for UFC 40: Vendetta. Nine years had passed since his epic battles in the first UFC in 1993, and it was almost six years since he last stepped into the Octagon. Many people thought they'd seen the last of the World's Most Dangerous Man—that he was past his prime. But as the thirty-eight-year-old fighter came into view, he showed no evidence that time had withered his menacing appearance or his desire to fight. His intense stare was that of a warrior who had entered hundreds of previous battles just to be prepared for this particular one. His chiseled physique spoke of a lifetime of training and preparation. It was the moment the fight world had been waiting for—the return of one of the sport's greatest legends.

Ken Shamrock's entrance into the first UFC happened by chance. While mindlessly flipping through an issue of *Black Belt* magazine in fall 1993, he came across a rather peculiar advertisement. Promoters of an event called the Ultimate Fighting Championship were looking for expert martial artists to compete in a full-contrast elimination tournament that had no weight classes or rules. He read the advertisement several times, and he couldn't help but smile. Such a tournament was designed for him.

Growing up in California's foster care system, Shamrock had learned how to wield his fists at a young age. He'd fought on the streets for his survival. He'd fought in juvenile hall for his honor.

With his heavy right hand, he had knocked out men twice his age behind bars and in various Toughman competitions. Over the years, he had even entered several full-contact karate tournaments to see what the hype was all about, but was disqualified because they said he punched too hard. After a lifetime of brawling, Shamrock doubted that traditional martial artists with their flashy punches, kicks, and blocks could handle the type of ferocity one learns on the street. And if they could, all he had to do was take them to the ground and submit them. For the past two years, he had been living in Japan and studying under the world's most experienced submission fighters, learning how to make an opponent

Royce Gracie throws a kick to the leg of Ken Shamrock.

Ken Shamrock uses Royce Gracie's gi to hold him in place. "My whole strategy going in was to wear him out," says Shamrock, "make him dog-assed tired to where he could hardly stand."

writhe in pain through various chokeholds and joint locks. He knew the techniques worked in an actual fight, because in Pancrase, a Japanese full-contact fighting event that allowed striking and grappling, he had used the techniques to defeat numerous opponents before thousands of fight fans.

With his impressive credentials, Shamrock had little trouble securing a spot in the event. On the night of November 12, 1993, only three days after competing in Japan, he arrived in Denver, Colorado, feeling confident that he would take home the first UFC's title belt.

Much like Shamrock had expected, the majority of his fellow competitors had devoted their lives to styles such as karate and tae kwon do. Backstage they warmed up with crescent kicks and ridge hand strikes, as sure of their skills as he had been when he first stepped onto the mats in Japan. Submitted by much smaller opponents, Shamrock had learned the hard way that it took more than just mental and physical toughness to make a successful fighter.

In his first bout of the night, Shamrock passed that lesson on to Patrick Smith, a kickboxer who had boasted earlier that he was immune to pain. In the opening seconds, Smith came forward and threw a kick to the leg. Shamrock shot in for a double-leg takedown, put the striker on the canvas, and then seized Smith's right leg and dropped back, applying a heel hook. In seconds, the kickboxer was in agony, and he pounded his hand in submission.

The bout had gone pretty much as Shamrock had anticipated. After a brief rest backstage, he climbed back into the Octagon to take on Royce Gracie, the only wildcard in the event. Shamrock had never before grappled with a competitor who studied Brazilian Jiu-Jitsu and wore a gi

(uniform), but after manhandling some of the best grapplers in the world in Japan, he felt confident that nothing Gracie could do would hurt him. Shamrock understood positioning, and he could spot a submission hold coming from a mile away.

A little over a minute into their bout, Shamrock had his opponent right where he wanted him—laying on his back in the middle of the Octagon. Feeling the time was right, he seized Gracie's right leg and dropped back to once again apply a heel hook. But immediately he knew something wasn't right. "He had wrapped his gi around my arm, so when I sat back, it basically pulled him up on top of me," said Shamrock. "Then I couldn't get my arm out of the gi to apply the heel hook. So I tried to turn on my side, and when I did, he wrapped his gi and his hand around my throat. I didn't feel there was any danger there because his other hand was tied up with mine. Then all of a sudden I felt this gi tighten around my neck. I was like, 'What the hell is that?'" Gasping for air, Shamrock realized it was only a matter of seconds before he would pass out, and he tapped in submission.

Shamrock handled his postfight interview with class, but inwardly he craved revenge. "I don't like losing, and for me to lose on national television was a hard thing to accept," said Shamrock. "Coming from the streets, I wasn't afraid of anything. I very rarely lost a fight, and when I did, I always came back and won. I always found a way to win. I needed to face him again for myself and to prove to all those people who watched the first event that I wasn't a quitter. I was used to fighting bare back, so I just needed to learn how to defend myself against someone wearing a gi (uniform). I wouldn't make the same mistakes twice."

Mounted on Christophe Leininger, Ken Shamrock fires away with punches. "I knew he was a great Judo guy, because he had been on the U.S. Team," says Shamrock. "I knew he had some pretty good skills, but I also knew that in the UFC skills didn't mean anything if you couldn't take a punch."

fights in order to meet each other in the finals. To achieve this, Shamrock defeated Christophe Leininger in his quarterfinal bout by trapping him against the fence and raining down punches. Then in the semifinals, he finished kickboxer Felix Lee Mitchell with a rear naked choke.

Shamrock waited backstage with the knowledge that his revenge was near and prepared himself mentally for the most important fight of his life. But just as he was beginning his warm-up routine, he received some devastating news. Gracie had thrown in the towel shortly after he stepped into the Octagon for his semifinal bout. Apparently, his struggle to defeat powerful street brawler Kimo Leopoldo in his first match of the night had taken its toll, and he could not continue.

Although Shamrock felt ready to take on Gracie only a few months after his loss, he would have to wait almost a year and a half for his redemption. While training for UFC 2: *No Way Out*, to be held on March 11, 1994, at Mammoth Gardens Event Center in Denver, Colorado, he blocked a high kick while sparring with a teammate and broke his hand. He still wanted to compete, but when doctors told him that he might never fight again if he injured his hand any further, he reluctantly withdrew from the show. Shamrock watched from the sidelines as Gracie took home the title belt yet again, and it fueled his rage. He entered UFC 3: *Revenge*, on September 9, 1994, at Independence Arena in Charlotte, North Carolina, prepared to give the Brazilian the fight of his life. Gracie, however, was on the opposite side of the quarterfinal bracket, which meant that they both had to win their first two

With Gracie out of the event, Shamrock was almost guaranteed a victory. All he had to do was step into the Octagon and defeat karate practitioner Harold Howard. But when organizers of the show called Shamrock's name, he told them that he wasn't coming out. He didn't care about the title belt or the prize money—he cared about beating Gracie. Having been robbed of his rematch yet again, he saw no reason to continue.

The fans of the sport were growing anxious to see the two warriors square off. To ensure that everyone got what they wanted, promoters decided to create the first ever Superfight in UFC 5: *Return of the Beast*. Instead of being a part of the tournament, Shamrock and Gracie would fight each other in a headlining bout.

The showdown was advertised in various media around the world, and on the night of April 7, 1995, Independence Arena in Charlotte, North Carolina, was packed to the brim with fight fans. "I didn't want to go out there and just beat Royce," said Shamrock. "I wanted to shut down his whole bragging system, which was, 'We're in better condition, our skills are better, and we can beat anybody, anywhere, anytime.' My whole strategy going in was to wear him out, make him dog-assed tired to where he could hardly stand. I was going to beat him—beat on his ribs, slowly break him down, and then treat him like a baby. I really wanted to embarrass the guy."

Shamrock's game plan worked well. He took Gracie to the ground, obtained the top position, and then pounded on his opponent's ribs and face for thirty minutes straight. Despite the abuse Gracie absorbed, he refused to tap in submission. This became a problem because at the time there weren't any judges and there was no way to determine a winner if one competitor refused to give in and submit. The fight had been scheduled for thirty minutes, but not wanting it to end in a draw, organizers of the show gave the warriors five extra minutes to see if one of them could pull out a victory. When neither fighter changed his strategy going into overtime, the referee made a judgment call and stood them up.

Shamrock used the opportunity to land two powerful punches to Gracie's face. "The reason why I was able to rock him was because I was wearing him down," said Shamrock. "I tried the same punch right in the beginning of the fight, but it didn't land. First time I missed it, but the second time he was worn out, a little bit slower,

and I hit it." After landing his shots, Shamrock brought the fight back to the canvas. He began delivering head butts and strikes, swelling up Gracie's already battered face. But Gracie weathered the abuse like a true champion, and the two combatants were eventually separated without a victor being declared.

Although Shamrock hadn't knocked Gracie out as he had wanted to, it was obvious to all those watching who had dominated from start to finish. Shamrock continued to rise in popularity because he did something no competitor had done before—go the distance with the jiu-jitsu master from Brazil. He fought in one Superfight after the next, defeating amateur wrestler Dan "The Beast" Severn with a guillotine choke in UFC 6: *Clash of the Titans*, held on July 14, 1995, at Casper Events Center in Casper, Wyoming, asserting his dominance over Oleg "The Russian Bear" Taktarov in UFC 7: *The Brawl in Buffalo*, held on September 8, 1995, at the Buffalo Memorial Auditorium in Buffalo, New York, and then captured the dangerous street fighter Kimo Leopoldo in a kneed bar at UFC 8: *David vs. Goliath*, held on February 16, 1996, in San Juan, Puerto Rico.

As Shamrock's victories accumulated, young athletes flooded to Lodi, California, in hopes of gaining entrance into his training facility, the Lion's Den, which he had started a few years earlier to train fighters who wanted to compete in Japan. Instead of teaching how to break boards and do katas like most martial arts studios in the United States, Shamrock taught how to fight while standing and on the ground.

Thousands of fighters wanted to train with him but Shamrock didn't accept just anyone. Not wanting to waste his time training guys who thought a crescent kick could be used in a real

Ken Shamrock
throws a right cross
at Tito Ortiz.

Ken
Shamrock
shoots on
Tito Ortiz.

Tito Ortiz lands a jab to the face of Ken Shamrock.

Tying Ken Shamrock up in the clinch, Tito Ortiz fires a series of knees to the midsection and face.

fight, he searched for those who were well-conditioned athletes rather than those who were experienced martial artists. To weed out the weak before they stepped foot into his gym, he created a tryout that consisted of eight hours of physical and mental abuse. It involved push-ups, sit-ups, miles of running, and grueling sparring sessions where Shamrock twisted their joints. "The test was not made for you to pass," said Shamrock. "It was made for you to want to quit. So by making you want to quit, it shows me the intensity or the will that you have to succeed."

Despite the high failure rate, over the course of many months, Shamrock managed to round up a small group of young men who had the heart, the desire, and the physical ability to learn what he had to teach them. Once they had made the team, Shamrock shaved their heads, moved them into his fighters' house, and then began the slow process of building them up from scratch. In exchange for his generosity, his students dedicated all their time and effort to training. They learned how to submit an opponent with arm bars, leg locks, heel hooks, and chokes. They learned how to punch, kick, and tie an opponent up in the clinch. They spent as many as six hours a day repeatedly drilling techniques; thus, it didn't take long before they could offer Shamrock the kind of resistance that he needed to stay in shape. "I was very hands on with them," said Shamrock. "I controlled the amount of time they put into training. I monitored the times they ate and the times they could go out. It was a real regimented deal, and it worked very well."

Shamrock didn't keep his fighters in the nest for long. Once he felt a student was ready to compete, he sent him over to Japan to get experience fighting in Pancrase events. And those who managed to rack up a number of victories over top competitors overseas soon followed Shamrock's lead into the UFC. This included Guy Mezger, Pete Williams, Jerry Bohlander, Mikey Burnett, and Frank Shamrock. Just like their instructor, they tore through the competition in the Octagon, making the Lion's Den the most respected and feared MMA fighting team in the world.

Shamrock became a leader in the sport of MMA. In the Octagon, he displayed sportsmanship and courage. Outside the ring, he frequently traveled the country to appear on talk shows, trying to convince the general public that the UFC was not a barbaric sport. But despite all his efforts to shed a positive light on MMA competition and its competitors, the UFC continued to attract negative attention. "The UFC was having a hard time," said Shamrock. "Every place we went, we were getting banned. At one event, we had to pack everything up the night before the show, charter two planes, and fly to another state just so we could make it happen."

Shamrock hoped that time would help solve the sport's problems. He continued to compete, but when he entered UFC 9: *Motor City Madness*, on May 17, 1996, in Detroit, Michigan, to defend his Superfight belt against Dan Severn for the second time, he was forced to make a moral decision that put a black mark on his nearly flawless record. "The show was held in Detroit, Michigan, and the night before the event the courts made it illegal for competitors to punch," said Shamrock. "Prior to that, there was a different show over in Canada that had the same thing happen to them. Competitors started punching, and they all got arrested after the show. The promoters told me not to worry about it, to go ahead and punch, and that they would fine me at a later date. I remember thinking about it, won-

A bloody Ken Shamrock refuses to give in to Tito Ortiz.

dering what to do. I thought about all the Juvenile Halls I had visited along the way, promoting the fact that they could do anything in life so long as they followed the rules and stayed within the guidelines. Growing up in group homes, I had learned that your team suffers when you foul, and your family suffers when you break the law. I had learned that the hard way, and I wasn't about to do that same thing again. I was being told that it was okay to break the rules, but it was totally against everything that I had promoted the UFC and myself to be about. And so, I chose not to punch. Because I chose not to punch, I lost the fight. Severn won because he landed more punches."

Shamrock made up for his lack of punches against Severn when he fought Brian Johnston in Ultimate Ultimate '96, held in Birmingham, Alabama on December 7, 1996. The fight card was filled with champions from past events, all heavy hitters, and the last man standing in the ring would not only be declared the best warrior of the night, but also the best warrior in the UFC. Shamrock wanted that title. He wanted it so bad, in fact, that shortly after slamming Johnston to the canvas and trapping him against the fence, he blew off the submissions and began punching his opponent full force in the face and skull. While in the fight, Shamrock felt little pain, but shortly after the referee pulled him off his devastated opponent, he felt pain shooting down his arm. When he got back to the dressing room, the doctors informed him that he had broken his hand and could not continue.

Shamrock wanted to be back on top of the pile, but the sport continued its downward spiral, and fighters' purses began to dwindle at every show. Shamrock had a family to support, along with a house full of fighters, so when the UFC showed no sign of making a dramatic comeback at any time soon, he decided to use the popularity he'd garnered in MMA competition to move over to the ranks of professional wrestling. The transition was not an easy one to make for Shamrock. He had a professional wrestling background, but few of his fellow wrestlers took notice of that. They honed in on the fact that he hurt people for a living, really hurt them, and few of them wanted to take a chance of getting a limb broken in the ring with him. Spending weeks, sometimes months, away from his family also was not easy, but it was a sacrifice he was willing to make to pay the bills, at least for the time being. With the leader of the Lion's Den away competing on weekly television, however, the once invincible group of fighters slowly fell from grace over the next several years. "The Lion's Den hasn't been the same because I didn't have the time to train the fighters," said Shamrock. "I had a system that worked, but when I went into the WWF, I wasn't able to be there and help them. Therefore, things kind of went downhill from there."

Just when the fight world thought they had seen the last of the Lion's Den glory, Shamrock decided to make a comeback in the UFC at UFC 40. "I was tired of running around all the time on the road with the WWF," said Shamrock. "I wanted to spend more time at home with my family and kids. I also wanted to get back into fighting because I realized I was running out of time to do that."

To get the training that he needed, Shamrock placed himself in the hands of his former students, and they brought him up to an acceptable level of performance on all the techniques that they had learned in his absence. Within months,

Shamrock felt ready to take on the world, and he signed a contract with the UFC to fight Tito Ortiz, the current light heavyweight champion, in UFC 40.

Shamrock had agreed to the match for two reasons: First, he wanted the light heavyweight championship belt. But more importantly, he felt he had a score to settle with the Huntington Beach Bad Boy. Back in March, 1999, Ortiz had defeated Lion's Den fighter Guy Mezger at UFC 19: *Ultimate Young Guns*, in Bay St. Louis, Mississippi. Instead of shaking Mezger's hand after the bout, Ortiz had put on a tee shirt that read, "Gay Mezger is my bitch." It was a blatant sign of disrespect for Shamrock and his crew of fighters, but Ortiz's assault didn't stop there. After strutting around the Octagon, he raised both his hands and dramatically flipped off the entire Lion's Den. Immediately, Shamrock leapt up onto the fence of the Octagon, fully prepared to set Ortiz straight. But before words turned into blows, the referee had intervened.

Time did little to ease the animosity. In the years that followed, Shamrock watched Ortiz evolve with the sport, taking on coaches in kickboxing, wrestling, grappling, boxing, and conditioning and bragging that he was the best warrior to ever step foot into the Octagon, as if he had invented the sport of MMA. In UFC 30: *Battle of the Boardwalk*, on February 24, 2001, in Atlantic City, he watched Ortiz pick up Evan Tanner, an accomplished grappler, and then slam him to the mat, knocking him out. In UFC 33: *Victory in Vegas*, on September 28, 2001, at the Mandalay in Las Vegas, he watched Ortiz put world-class wrestler Vladimir "The Janitor" Matyushenko on his back, and then he beat him senseless over the course of five rounds. Shamrock watched Ortiz dominate everyone he stepped into the Octagon

Showing his sportsmanship, Ken Shamrock lifts the hand of Tito Ortiz.

with, and yet he still felt the young fighter had one more very important lesson to learn—respect for those who had come before him and paved the way. If it hadn't been for Royce Gracie and himself, the only two competitors in the early UFCs who had understood the importance of grappling, the UFC would never have amounted to anything more than a glorified Toughman contest. Competitors such as Ortiz would never have had the chance to bask in the spotlight.

Shamrock felt confident nothing could stop him from defeating Ortiz, but then he tore ligaments in his knee during practice. "I figured I could

overcome it, get in there and win the fight," said Shamrock. "I really thought I could beat Tito Ortiz with one leg. Training was hard, because I couldn't run. I was forced to cut back on my training because my knee swelled up. I should have just called it a day so I could come back another time, but I was just too hardheaded. I had always been able to overcome any injury, and I thought I would be able to do it again." Shamrock trained when he could, and despite constant pain, he made the trip to Las Vegas to see how his skills fared against the new and improved Ortiz.

It was the most anticipated match the UFC

had experienced in its nine-year history, and as the two warriors took their positions inside the Octagon, millions of fans around the world found themselves wondering what the outcome would be. Would the legend of the past be able to pull out a victory, or would the champion of the present run through this competitor just like he had all the rest?

The capacity crowd was on its feet as the fight got underway. Shamrock came forward with confidence, but he soon realized his injury was not something he should have taken so lightly. He didn't have the mobility that he needed to pivot, shoot, or struggle for position on the ground. This allowed Ortiz to get the upper hand right from the start.

When the two fighters tore into each other on their feet, Ortiz tied Shamrock up in a clinch and delivered knee after knee to his midsection and face. Shamrock retaliated with a host of uppercuts, but his punches didn't possess their former ferocity. It looked as if Ortiz were immune to Shamrock's blows until he was caught with a hook. Ortiz's legs buckled, and he brought the fight to the ground. Once Ortiz recuperated, he took the top position and delivered knees to Shamrock's body and elbows to his face. Shamrock defended as best he could, but when he managed to work back to his feet, his eyes were badly swollen and dripping blood.

Ortiz's dominance grew more complete as the minutes passed. He dismantled Shamrock with an array of strikes. He took the fighting legend to the ground at will, scooted him over to the fence, and worked to enlarge the gashes on his face. By the third round, many people thought Shamrock was going to throw in the towel. He

had taken so much abuse that his shots were straying way off target, while Ortiz continued to fire straight, accurate punches.

Shamrock might not have brought his former strength, stamina, or technique into the Octagon, but he had come armed with all the courage in the world. There was little doubt he would have kept fighting until the end of the bout, but fortunately the referee put a stop to the abuse at the end of the third round. "I really thought I could beat Tito Ortiz with one leg, and I was wrong," said Shamrock. "I couldn't shoot. I couldn't do submissions because I needed both of my legs to squeeze and get into position. I really couldn't punch well because I couldn't pivot or turn my punches over. So my injury hindered me from doing a lot of things that I should have been able to do. But that was my responsibility. I took the fight knowing that I was hurt, thinking that I would be able to overcome those things, and I paid the consequences. Tito was better prepared, and I got beat by a better fighter."

Despite losing the fight and passing the torch on to the new generation, Shamrock had no plans of leaving the sport at any time soon. He had knee surgery, and once he recovered, he began training as he had in the past. "MMA competition has put me in a situation where I can walk through life being proud of who I am and what I have accomplished," said Shamrock. "Without it, I don't know what I would have done. I fell in love with it the first time I stepped into the ring, and I have never looked back. We all went through a hard time when politics got involved and the sport was banned, but because we loved what we did, loved where it was going, we stuck with it."

The Ronin

Jiu-jitsu expert Carlos Newton entered UFC 40 on November 22, 2002, eager for redemption. His previous two fights in the Octagon had been against world-class wrestler Matt Hughes for the welterweight title belt, and he had suffered the sting of defeat on both occasions. Newton still felt he was one of the best fighters in the world, and he was confident that he could reclaim the title belt Hughes had stolen from him during their first encounter. But before he could get another shot at the title, he first had to take out Pete Spratt, a Thai boxer who possessed an arsenal of deadly punches and kicks.

Newton's game plan was simple—take his opponent to the ground, obtain the top position, and then move from one submission hold to the next until he found one that Spratt couldn't block. Although many people felt such a strategy was outdated considering the quality of current competitors, Newton executed it with the same perfection Royce Gracie had years earlier. When Spratt threw a kick in the opening seconds, Newton rushed forward, picked him up, and then slammed him down. Hovering over his thrashing opponent, he isolated Spratt's arm and twisted it painfully back, forcing Spratt to tap in submission. In less than two minutes, Newton had reminded all the wrestlers and strikers who currently ruled the Octagon why jiu-jitsu experts such as he were as dangerous as ever.

Growing up in the British Virgin Islands, Carlos Newton had always been the top student in his class. When he turned ten years old, his single mother realized he would never receive the type of schooling that he needed on the islands, and thus, she reluctantly sent him to Canada by himself to continue his education. Being all alone in a new country at such a young age was not easy for Newton. "There was a period there where I thought anything could happen to me. I didn't always have a place to stay, but studying jiu-jitsu really helped me," said Newton. "I would travel to a bunch of different dojos around the country by bus, and it suited me pretty well. . . . I approached every learning experience I had like a baby. I didn't react to egos. When a person was actually able to beat me, I always clung to that person on the mat. I did not care at all about winning; it was just sheer pursuit of learning the art in every facet."

Newton decided to name his unique style of fighting after the popular Japanese cartoon *Dragon Ball Z* after he had acquired a wide variety of techniques from a number of different disciplines.

Carlos Newton giving the crowd a show.

"The reason I took the name from the cartoon is because they kept it true to the nature of what it means to be a fighter," said Newton. "I like what it stands for, and I try to be a role model for kids. If I was ever going to name my style anything, it was going to be something that would get kids interested in the martial arts."

Over the years, Newton took home one trophy after another in karate point sparring matches and kata demonstrations, but eventually he wanted to see how his skills fared in actual combat. "My first professional [mixed martial arts] MMA event was when I turned nineteen— I fought Jean Riviere in an Extreme Fighting show in Montreal," said Newton. "I weighed 180 pounds, and he weighed 286. We really rock and rolled. I got exhausted, and pretty much tapped out. I almost passed out. . . . But I pretty much

controlled the position throughout the fight, and so it caught the public's attention that I would do that well with such a big weight advantage to my opponent. He had fought in the Brazil show and he knocked out all his opponents. I was the only guy who walked out of there in one piece."

Not only did Newton catch the public's attention with his impressive professional debut, but he also caught the attention of promoters. A short while later, he began competing in Japan on a regular basis. "That's where they started calling me Ronin because the Japanese community knew that my fighting idol was Musashi, who was a famous Ronin," said Newton. "He won sixty-four duels to the death. I felt that there was a greater sense of the martial arts spirit in Japan, the Budo, and it was a great honor to be able to compete over there. When I fought there, I

Carlos Newton throws a jab at Pat Miletich.

Pat Miletich throws a Thai kick at Carlos Newton's midsection.

wouldn't come straight home. I would always travel the country and train at different places."

Newton continued to acquire new skills, and after he'd accumulated a large number of victories over top competitors, he was invited to compete in UFC 17: *Redemption*, the middleweight elimination tournament, held on May 15, 1998, at the Mobile Civic Center in Mobile, Alabama.

In his first bout of the night, Newton defeated his opponent Bob Gilstrap with a triangle choke in just fifty seconds, and then he stepped back into the Octagon to take on world-class wrestler

Carlos Newton in Pat Miletich's guard, looking for a submission.

Dan Henderson. The battle went back and forth, up and down. When Newton couldn't land a submission, he went toe-to-toe on his feet and broke his opponent's jaw. "I ducked to the side and hit him with a body shot," said Newton. "I knew that I had hurt him, and I came upstairs right away. I heard his jaw go 'crack.' I looked at my hand, thinking it was my hand. I had broken his jaw, and he just did the Ickey Shuffle and came right back. I wasn't sure what happened, and then my coaches told me to get him." Newton beat up his opponent to try to put him away, but Henderson seemed immune to pain. The bout went the distance, and the judges awarded Henderson a split decision.

Newton decided to take some time off after the loss. His long-term goal was to become an orthopedic surgeon, and he needed to maintain a high grade point average in college in order to be accepted into medical school. But he quickly realized he would only be hurting himself by staying away from the martial arts. "I feel that my schoolwork and training for fights complement one another," said Newton. "School keeps me focused. Fighting and training give me discipline. You need both. I found that my fighting skills improved when I was going to school full time, and I felt my school work improved when I started to reflect on my fighting career."

Despite being bogged down with his studies, Newton found the time to train every day, and soon his competitive spirit brought him back to the Octagon in UFC 31, where he would take on Pat Miletich for the welterweight title. "I tried to see it as just another fight," said Newton, "and not get carried away because it was a big title match—didn't want to screw up my head. I tried not to think the fight was going to put me on top of the pile and keep me there for a while. I just wanted to go out there and do a good job. . . .

Carlos Newton secures a headlock that forces Pat Miletich to tap in submission.

He's such an experienced fighter. For me, still growing up as a fighter, experience is what I fear most. I don't care about the young guys like myself who can do ten back flips. Experience and brains always overcomes brawn. I felt Pat, if anything, would have more of that than I do. I counted on that."

Both fighters came out striking, and it wasn't until the middle of the third round that Newton found an opening. As Miletich advanced with punches, Newton shot beneath them and executed a flawless double-leg takedown. On the canvas, he began scooting Miletich toward the fence to rob him of mobility. To defend, Miletich turned a hip and tried to scoot out from underneath, but in the process he gave his back. Newton flipped around to the side and secured Miletich in a headlock. In a matter of seconds, Miletich tapped in submission.

Newton had stolen the welterweight title belt from one of the most successful combatants to ever step into the Octagon. Using this momentum, he entered UFC 34 on November 2, 2001, to defend his title against Matt Hughes, a world-class wrestler known for his power slams.

The fight went back and forth for the first five-minute round. Both had amazing takedowns, and both had crafty escapes. But with neither of them landing any serious shots, the fight was still not yet decided. In the opening of the second round, however, Hughes got busy. He closed the distance, picked Newton up, and then power slammed him to the mat. When they landed, Newton captured Hughes in his guard, grabbed one of the wrestler's outstretched arms, and wrapped his legs around his head, locking him in a triangle choke. Things did not look good for Hughes, but he still had one more trick up his sleeve. Displaying his tremendous strength, he picked Newton up off the mat and carried him on his shoulders over to the fence.

Carlos Newton holds a triangle choke tight. When Matt Hughes slams him to the canvas, both will be unconscious. "I feel it was a tough break," says Newton. "I felt like I was too good of a boy and should have just held onto the fence and not took the slam."

Although Newton found himself five feet off the ground with his back against the fence, he kept his legs wrapped tightly around Hughes' head. He could feel the wrestler slowly losing consciousness, and he was sure victory would be his. In a final attempt to save himself, however, Hughes once again power slammed Newton to the mat.

When the two of them hit the canvas, they were both knocked unconscious. Newton had been knocked out from the fall, and Hughes had passed out from the chokehold. The referee came close to inspect the situation, and the first thing he saw was that Newton wasn't moving, and so the referee called the fight in Hughes' favor. "I felt like I was just too good of a boy and should have just held onto the fence and not took the slam," said Newton. "I should have held on, because I knew he was passing out. And he did pass out! When I hit, the first thing I thought was, 'Oh, that was hard.' I must have thought that at the same time I was going out. Then I was coming to. I asked John (the referee) who had won, and he told me I lost. I thought, 'How can that be?' It was not the type of disappointment where you felt like you've let yourself down— you just feel like it was a tough break. It was like flipping a coin; that's what it felt like."

Despite this, Newton wasted no time getting back into training. "I have come to learn that you get from life what you give," said Newton. "If you give your training your all, you are going to get something out of it. I always remember that I do it for me. I practiced martial arts long before I ever entered the Octagon. I had always wanted to be a great fighter, and this is a way of helping me achieve that dream. I just keep my head on, and life goes by one day at a time."

Pete Spratt throws a kick to the leg of Carlos Newton. "I found myself up against the number two ranked fighter in the world," says Spratt. "It was only my second appearance, and so I was just a little bit nervous."

Carlos Newton wrenches the arm of Pete Spratt to secure a Kimura. "I didn't expect him to be so strong," says Spratt. "When he got me down, I couldn't move."

SECTION TWO

The Wrestlers

The Beast and the Hammer

On the night of April 7, 1995, the fight world experienced yet another unexpected surprise. Dan Severn and Dave Beneteau, two amateur wrestlers, had made it to the finals of UFC 5. Instead of coming out and attacking each other with punches, kicks, and crafty submission holds, they locked up in the center of the Octagon, grappling for a superior position. This went on for several minutes until Severn brought his opponent down by hooking a leg, a move straight out of wrestling 101. And when the fight went to the canvas, there were no fancy chokeholds or ankle locks. Other than throwing an occasional head butt and slap to the face, Severn primarily worked to keep his opponent on his back, almost as if he were trying to pin him. The only thing that resembled past UFC fights was the arm lock Severn slapped on Beneteau, forcing him to submit. But overall, it looked more like a wrestling match than a true fight. Little did anyone know, the era of the wrestler had just begun.

While karate and kung fu practitioners were desperate to learn how to fight on the ground during the early years of the UFC, few of them considered taking up wrestling. They all wanted to study Brazilian Jiu-Jitsu because, just like the eastern fighting styles, it was shrouded in mystery. Wrestling just wasn't foreign enough. It was taught in every high school and college around the country. In order to learn the discipline, a student didn't have to bow to a teacher, wear a gi (uniform), or go through a series of rituals or tests before they were given the most advanced techniques. If someone wanted to discover how to wrestle, all that person had to do was accept the challenge.

There were a select few, however, who understood that the moves and techniques of wrestling could be used quite effectively in a true fight. "I had always thought wrestling was America's form of the martial arts," said Mike Murphy, the executive director of the International Wrestling Museum. "It came over with the Pilgrims and swept down the West Coast. The Institute of War Camps taught it to soldiers, and it was used in battle. Wrestling was not just for sport, it had always been an effective form of fighting, but before the UFC there were only a handful of people who saw it like I did."

One person who understood the ferocity of wrestling technique was Dan Severn. After "wrecking shop" on the mats of Arizona State University, he had set out to become the best amateur wrestler in the world, and between 1982 and 1994, he had seized over a dozen national

Dan Severn riles up the crowd. "I never thought of wrestling as a martial art," says Severn. "I just went out there as a wrestler and a competitor. It's a whole different mindset."

and international titles. Severn now felt that he had accomplished most of his goals in the sport and began searching for a way to support his family by using the skills he had learned on the mat. "I looked at the UFC, and I saw this 180-pound Brazilian was doing pretty good with this grappling stuff," said Severn. "I thought I was a pretty darn good wrestler, and they are pretty similar. I've competed all over the world simply to step up to the podium to be given a medal or a trophy or a plaque or simply to be declared the best wrestler that day. Now if you wave a belt under my nose and a few bucks, I'm good to go."

Severn filled out an application and sent it in. He was thrilled to learn that the promoters of the UFC were already considering bringing an amateur wrestler into the mix. Although the first three shows had been a resounding success, the event had been blasted in the press as being a blood sport. They thought bringing a competitor in from a legitimate sport such as amateur wrestling might add some credibility to the UFC.

To take the next step, Severn met with the promoters in Las Vegas, Nevada, and gave them a little demonstration of his skill. He told them he could handle the competition even though he had never been in a fistfight in his life. But before he left the meeting, Severn could already tell that he wasn't what they were looking for. He was thirty-six years old, almost a decade past his prime. He might have weighed well over two hundred pounds, but his physique was anything but chiseled. He went home thinking that he would never hear from them again, but then months later, he received a call. "I think someone who was supposed to be in it ended up getting hurt," said Severn, "because by the time I was told I was in it, I only had about five days to prepare."

Severn accepted the challenge even though he understood that the tournament had only two rules, no biting or gouging, and that he would have to win three bouts in a single night to take home the prize money. Few martial arts practitioners could have prepared themselves mentally or physically on such short notice, but Severn wasn't worried. While the other competitors in the event were preparing for a fight, he was preparing for a competition—something he had

been doing day in and day out for the past twenty years. "A fighter has to conjure up animosity," said Severn. "If you look at professional boxers, they have to conjure up all these feeling of hatred before they step into the ring. As a competitor, you just give me the rules, no matter how few or many there might be, and I'm going to go out there and compete."

When Severn's opponents tried to punch or kick him in the face, he would snatch them off their feet and then deposit them very roughly on the canvas. Once he had them on the ground, their natural instincts would be to turn over to their stomach and try to stand back up again. That's when he would take their head and "crank" it to the side or seize a limb and twist it in a direction it didn't want to go. He might take a couple of blows in the process, but that was to be expected. "Wrestlers have been conditioned by fifteen years of wrestling and battle," said Murphy. "They are so used to this kind of combat that it becomes a part of whom they are. They

As Dan Severn struggles for position, Royce Gracie lands an elbow to the back of the head.

just spend hours and hours in combative situations, allowing almost everything except kicking and punching. They've learned how to focus in this kind of competition."

The big question mark in Severn's mind was Royce Gracie. The man could do some amazing

Matt Hughes, a powerful wrestler, works to keep the top position on Carlos Newton.

things in the Octagon, things Severn had never seen in all his years of wrestling. But one thing he knew unquestionably was that he wouldn't fall victim to a chokehold or arm bar as easily as the karate practitioners Gracie had faced in the past. If he knew anything, it was how to protect himself on the ground. Everything was about positioning, always being aware of his center of gravity, as well as his opponents. He would force Gracie to work, and in the process, he would most likely wear him down. "If you watch how some of the better collegiate wrestling teams practice, it is mind-boggling what these people

do," said Severn. "Takedowns are the easy part of practice. To develop cardiovascular strength, you do what is known as The Grind—a wrestler gets down on all fours, in the referee's position, and has thirty seconds to get someone off his back and then climb back to his feet. They'll make you do that over and over again, with four or five guys."

After being pushed like this for years in practice, Severn was pretty sure that he could outlast almost anyone on the ground. He kept in top shape year round, but in order to squeak in a little additional training, he spent the five days leading up to the event with professional wrestler Al Snow. "He has a martial arts background, as well as some of the other professional wrestlers there at his school," said Severn. "So they would throw on boxing gloves and play the game, 'Punch Dan.' Basically, we just kept moving around, go into a clinch, a takedown, or a throw down, something like that. I really wish I'd taken footage of it because it would have made for some great slapstick comedy. It was really comical training. I really didn't know what to expect. Being in wrestling my whole life, I had never really practiced to strike another human being. So my game plan was to work the clinch, go for the takedown, and then slap them on the side of the head to get people to submit."

Wrestler Matt Hughes, having studied jiu-jitsu, struggles to submit Frank Trigg with a guillotine choke.

Severn was eager to find out how his wrestling skills would fare in a true fight, and on the night of December 16, 1994, in Tulsa Oklahoma, for UFC 4: *Revenge of the Warriors*, he learned the answer when he stepped into the Octagon with Anthony "Mad Dog" Macias, a kickboxer who boasted having devastating knockout power in his strikes. When Macias came forward and attempted to land a kick, Severn closed the gap between them, took his opponent's back, and then wrapped his arms tightly around his midsection. While trying to figure out what to do next, Severn was hit with a reverse elbow in the side of his head. Never before had he been hit so hard, and it answered one of his greatest concerns—do I have what it takes to compete in this kind of event? "People ask me how to know if they are ready to compete in [mixed martial arts] MMA, and I tell them they have to take a shot," said Severn. "That is the ultimate test. Because once you take a shot,

and your television screen gets all disrupted, you break down into autopilot. Whether that is a good or bad thing, that autopilot will kick in. One of two things will happen—flight or fight. You will either engage or you will disengage. That's it. It's one of the most ugly tests to undergo."

When Severn's autopilot kicked on, it told him to do one thing—dispense with his opponent. Cinching his arms tighter around Macias's midsection, Severn hefted his opponent over his shoulder and slammed him head first into the canvas. "He started getting back to his feet, and I couldn't believe he was going to crawl into it again," said Severn. "He came up, and then I threw him again. He hit with a lot more force than the first time, because I had his weight and my weight moving in the same direction. He hit harder that second time, and all I remember was we were both facedown on the mat, with me on top of him. I saw blood dripping on the canvas."

Hefting Hayato Sakurai off his feet, Matt Hughes carries his opponent on his shoulder before slamming him to the canvas.

Lying on top of his injured opponent, Severn struggled to put him away. He had mentally prepared himself to strike his opponents to win the competition, but now that he was being called to do so, he found it nearly impossible. Having competed for so many years in amateur wrestling, a sport where you are trained never to strike an opponent, he just couldn't do it. So he tried twisting Macias's face to the side. Next he tried smothering him. When nothing seemed to work, he wrapped his arm around Macias's neck and dug his forearm deep into his windpipe. Macias gurgled for a moment, and then tapped in submission.

Severn didn't have lightning-fast punches or kicks; as a matter of fact, he possessed no striking ability whatsoever. But in his first UFC match he had proven, just as Royce Gracie had proven, that strikes weren't necessary to finish off an opponent. This did not shock the spectators in the crowd or those watching on pay-per-view because they had learned about the effectiveness of ground fighting in the past three events. What came as a shock was that Severn had won without the aid of Brazilian Jiu-Jitsu or submission holds. He had won by utilizing the techniques of amateur wrestling, a discipline that was taught all over the United States. When he won his second bout of the evening in a similar fashion as his first, the announcers gave him the nickname "The Beast."

It wasn't until Severn entered the finals with Royce Gracie that the limitations of wrestling were exposed. Much like in his previous bouts, Severn took his opponent to the ground and obtained the top position. "I didn't strike anyone in my first two matches," said Severn. "I stuck just to wrestling technique. It wasn't a few minutes into my fight with Royce that I actually started to throw some kind of strikes. I said it time and again, I was struggling more with my conscience than I was with my opponent."

The match became a stalemate. Because of Severn's knowledge of positioning, Royce couldn't land the submissions that had come so easily with opponents in the past. And with Severn being limited to wrestling technique, which primarily focused on pinning his opponent rather than hurting him, he had no idea what do with Gracie, a master grappler who refused to fall victim to his rudimentary submissions. It wasn't until fifteen uneventful minutes had passed that Gracie caught the break he had been waiting for. With Severn hovering over him, he managed to bring up his legs, wrap them around Severn's head, and apply a triangle choke. Severn had no idea what was going on, but feeling himself slowly losing consciousness, he tapped in submission.

Randy Couture struggles to bring Pedro Rizzo, a powerful striker, to the mat.

Randy Couture smothers Tito Ortiz.

Despite losing in the finals, Severn had enjoyed the entire experience. Now knowing what he had to work on, he immediately jumped into training. He learned how to strike a downed opponent with his fists, knees, and elbows. He learned how to crank on an opponent's arms and legs and execute all the chokeholds that had been outlawed in wrestling. By the time he entered UFC 5, he had overcome his hesitation to punch a fellow competitor, and at the end of the evening, he took home the title belt. "Dan Severn elevated the entire sport of amateur wrestling by showing that its techniques are a form of martial art that can actually compete, equally if not at a higher level, than the other martial arts," said Murphy. "I think a lot of wrestlers felt that, but I don't think the general martial arts world felt that because of the power or mysticism that surrounded fighters such as Bruce Lee or Chuck Norris."

Once again the martial arts world had been flipped upside down. Instead of jiu-jitsu stylists flooding into the MMA scene, it was a host of amateur wrestlers who had been inspired by Severn's dominance in the Octagon. "Wrestling isn't like boxing or kickboxing, where they can go into professional careers after being an amateur," said Severn. "Wrestlers have high school and college, but there is nothing afterwards. There is no NFL or NHL. There is no true profession for an amateur wrestler. But now, with the UFC, they have a showcase. Now wrestlers can go into MMA and make a livelihood."

Severn had begun the era of the wrestler, erasing any doubt as to the effectiveness of the age-old discipline when, on December 16, 1995, he won the UFC: *Ultimate Ultimate 95* in Denver, Colorado, a tournament filled with champions of previous tournaments. Thousands of MMA competitors who had focused all their attention on learning jiu-jitsu now began integrating wrestling into their style. While they were playing catch-up, Mark "The Hammer" Coleman, a former Olympic amateur wrestler, took the torch from Severn and began his reign in the Octagon. On July 12, 1996, in Birmingham, Alabama, he won UFC 10: *The Tournament,* by grounding his opponents and then destroying them with hammering fists and head butts until the referee pulled him off. The game plan worked so well for him, in fact, that he decided to keep it. On February 7, 1997, in UFC 12: *Judgment Day,* he took on none other than Dan Severn, and after placing The Beast on his back and softening him up with slaps to the side of the head, he secured a headlock that forced Severn to tap. The victory awarded Coleman with a prestigious title—the first ever UFC heavyweight champion of the world.

It wasn't until UFC 14, on July 27, 1997, when he lost a decision to Maurice Smith, an accomplished striker who had learned how to sprawl, that Coleman realized there were holes in his strategy. "In the beginning, I just used my athletic ability, my wrestling skills, and my instincts, and I just went out there and kicked some ass," said Coleman. "I would just take my guys down and then head butt them. That was my game, and

it worked very well. But then the quality of opponents got so much better, and it made everything a completely different ball game. I had to learn how to fight them. You have to have a strategy. You have to conserve, control your breathing. Today you have to train hard, because the guy across from you most likely is. In wrestling, the man who works harder is usually able to squeak out the victory, and the same is true in MMA."

Severn came to the same realization. "I talk a lot about the early UFC and what it has evolved into," said Severn. "Everyone back then was one dimensional, and so was I. But I was a wrestler, which teaches you body mechanics and body control. I understood how leverage works, and I was able to use my techniques to get my victories at that time. Ground and pound, as ugly and barbaric as it is, is very effective. Stand-up fighters don't want to be on the ground, looking up and getting thumped on. They need that space in order to strike, and so they started learning how to avoid the takedown. I knew I had holes in my armor from the beginning, but the strikers really forced me to work on them. I began boxing and kickboxing three days a week. Granted, it's still a weakness in my armor, but at least I've acquired some survival skills. Everyone started doing the same thing, and it led to this metamorphosis. Now you have wrestlers that are phenomenal strikers, and you have strikers that are phenomenal wrestlers."

Although both Severn and Coleman suffered several defeats as the level of competition increased, they taught other amateur wrestlers who were thinking about entering the MMA competition just what they had to learn to survive. One competitor who took these lessons to heart was Randy Couture. He became perhaps the most decorated fighter the UFC had ever seen.

The Natural

Before entering a competition, whether it was wrestling or mixed martial arts (MMA), Randy Couture had always been big on studying his opponents. So while preparing to fight Maurice Smith for the heavyweight title belt at UFC: Ultimate Japan 1, *on December 21, 1997, in Yokohama, Japan, he sat down and watched a videotape of Smith's last battle, which happened to be against Mark Coleman. Couture examined how Smith timed his punches and kicks in order to avoid being taken to the ground. He analyzed how Coleman eventually brought the fight to the canvas and how Smith defended himself and escaped back to his feet. As the rounds passed, Couture saw the little tricks Smith used to frustrate Coleman, wear him down, and then force the wrestler to use all his willpower just to stay in the fight. After twenty-one minutes of battle, Couture knew exactly why Smith had been awarded a unanimous decision from the judges.*

The videotape told him one thing—Smith was the beginning of a new era, one where strikers were a dominant force. The wrestlers' heyday that Severn and Coleman had enjoyed for so long had come to an end. Couture understood that he would have to rely on more than ground and pound to remain competitive. Instead of finding this fact depressing, it lifted his spirits. If there was one thing Couture thrived on, it was a good challenge.

Randy Couture had been born to wrestle. He had become so addicted to the one-on-one nature of the sport in high school that after he graduated he decided to join the army in order to continue with his career. "That was where I really got my first taste of competitive wrestling, world-class training, and what it takes to compete at that level," said Couture. "Basically all I ever did was wrestle for the service. I hardly ever wore a uniform. My last three years in the military I was assigned to the sports department, and wrestling was basically my job. So,

as far as the military went, I pretty much had it made. I went to all the national training camps and national tournaments. It was a great place to compete for a guy with a family who had needs to be met as far as money, but still wanted to compete. It was a perfect situation. I got some national recognition that I didn't have coming out of high school that allowed me to get a scholarship and go to college."

After the army, Couture got busy on the mats at Oklahoma State for four years, and when that chapter of his life was over, he continued to com-

Randy Couture lands a
knee to the midsection of
fellow wrestler Kevin
Randleman.

pete on both a national and an international level. In the coming years, he won a gold medal in the 1991 Pan Am Games and won the U.S. Nationals on two separate occasions. But with a family to support, the income he earned on the wrestling circuit just wasn't enough. Not wanting to abandon the sport, he struggled to find a way to pay the bills while doing what he loved. That's when he began thinking about entering the UFC. "I was never in a lot of street fights growing up," said Couture. "It happened a couple of times, but it wasn't a regular part of my life. I was generally pretty easy going, and I talked real well so I didn't find myself in a lot of trouble. But I never thought of MMA competition as a fight. I just saw it as a competition similar to wrestling. It's a very physical competition, but it wasn't about the same kind of emotional feelings that you get when you think of fighting."

Despite his unique point of view, it wasn't the best time for another wrestler to enter the big show. After years of dominating in the Octagon, wrestlers such as Coleman were having a hard time with competitors who had learned how to sprawl, and they had paid a painful price in several of their matches. But Couture felt he could bring something to the sport that no other wrestler competing in the UFC had before. Both Severn and Coleman had focused primarily on freestyle wrestling; Couture was a master at Greco-Roman. "I think most styles of wrestling are good basis for MMA, but each has a different emphasis," said Couture. "Obviously to be able to change levels, penetrate, and take your opponent to the ground from the open, which is what a freestyle wrestler would be more adept at, is a nice skill to have. But with a lot of the guys learning to stop open takedowns, sprawl, and defend the open shots a lot better, a wrestler needs to have the ability to tie a guy up in the clinch, and then take him down from the clinch, which is what Greco-Roman is all about."

Randy Couture, showing his versatility, throws a kick to the leg of Pedro Rizzo, a world-class striker.

Couture began studying Greco-Roman wrestling while in the service, mainly because that was what his coach had always done. At the time, only a handful of competitors focused on this style. Receiving professional coaching on a daily basis, Couture quickly found himself one of the top Greco-Roman wrestlers in the country. "That was where I started, in the service, and it carried through college," said Couture. "I started winning national titles when I was in college. I think because no one else was really doing that, it was a challenge for me as an American to try to be a world champion in a less popular style. So that is what intrigued me, and I just always liked it."

Liking it was one thing, but trying to apply his skills in a UFC bout was something else entirely. There had been a reason why Severn and Coleman had focused on freestyle. They could shoot on their opponent from a distance, close the gap between them, and then take them to the ground

without being punched or kicked. For Couture to take an opponent down from the clinch, he would have to walk head on into their arsenal of strikes. Couture, however, didn't see it as a problem. He saw it as a way to test his stand-up skills. "I wanted to box when I was in junior high school," said Couture. "A local boxer, who ended up going to the Olympics, boxed at the Elks Club in Linwood, Oregon. I was sneaking over there and trying to box, and my mom found out about it and actually made me quit. It was the only sport she ever tried to keep me out of. And so that was my first exposure to it. Then, when I was in my advanced training in Fort Rutgers, Alabama, they had a boxing smoker, basically a small competition between the air traffic controllers, the air traffic mechanics, and the trainee helicopter pilots. I trained for about three weeks with a coach to get ready for that competition, but I never got paired up for a match. So I did a

Randy Couture finishes off Pedro Rizzo with a series of elbows to the face. "I didn't show up in the ring that night," says Rizzo. "All my movement was trying to avoid Randy, so I didn't land any punches or kicks."

lot of training, sparring, but I never got to compete. That was the extent of my boxing before the UFC. But it was always something I was interested in."

Before Couture invested too much time working on his striking, however, he first wanted to see if the promoters of the UFC would allow him to compete in the event. "I had been trying to get in for about nine months," said Couture. "Mark Coleman was the champ, and Don Frye was just on his way out of the UFC. There were several wrestlers competing in the UFC, and they put me

off. They thought they had enough wrestlers, and they didn't need any more. As it happened, I was training in Puerto Rico at the Pan Am Championships and competing there, and I got a call just two weeks away from UFC 13. Someone had hurt his hand who was supposed to be in the heavyweight tournament. They couldn't find anybody to take the fight on such short notice, and so I said that I would."

Much like Severn's first fight, Couture had only a short time to prepare for the event. Knowing he could not improve on his strikes in just two weeks, he spent his time learning how to defend against submissions. Other than that, he prepared as he would for any high-level wrestling tournament. "I had no training at all," said Couture. "I kind of got into it at the last minute, and it wasn't until after that first heavyweight tournament that I started the process of cross-training and adding the other skills I thought I needed to be a complete fighter. I kind of approached the sport similarly both mentally and physically to wrestling. I had learned a lot of things in wrestling that definitely applied to the fight game, such as breaking down technique and analyzing my opponents. I did, however, find it interesting that when I got into MMA I wasn't nervous, and I got real nervous for wrestling matches. That was a hard thing for me to understand. People would ask me, 'What do you mean, you get more nervous for a wrestling match when your opponents in the UFC can kick you in the head?' It didn't make any sense, but I think it came down to what my expectations were. I had a lot of expectations from myself in wrestling. I had a lot of goals and things I wanted to accomplish. When I first got into MMA, it was just something that I wanted to try for fun."

At UFC 13: *The Ultimate Force*, held on May 30,

with him—he is a much better boxer than I will ever think of being. He's a great kickboxer in my opinion, and so every time he tried to kick me, I wanted to put him on the ground. I wanted to make him pay for kicking me. Fortunately, I think the format in those times—the straight fifteen minutes, with two three-minute overtimes—

Mounted on top of Randy Couture, Ricco Rodriguez tries to capture his opponent's arm.

I really only had to take him down three times. And I don't think he had done a whole bunch of cross-training as far as defending takedowns or anything at that point. He learned how to survive on the ground, but he didn't really learn how to stop any takedowns or keep the fight on his feet."

Couture had won his battle with Smith by a majority decision, but his reign in the Octagon was not long lived. Shortly after earning the title belt from Smith, the sport began to feel the effects of the cable ban. Promoters of the show were forced to cut fighters' purses, so Couture decided

to abandon his title belt and take some time off from the UFC to refocus his attention on wrestling. He kept an eye on the competitors in the UFC, however, and he realized that if he was ever going to make a comeback, he was going to have to plug the holes in his fighting style. "When I took time out of the fight game, I determined that being on the bottom, fighting from my guard, was probably the weakest area of my game," said Couture, "and so I studied grappling and put myself in the bottom position a whole bunch in the year and a half that I took off."

Those skills would prove beneficial. When the sport started regaining its momentum, Couture decided to contact the UFC. He was surprised that they agreed to allow him back into the event, but he was even more surprised when they gave him a chance at reclaiming the heavyweight title belt immediately. In UFC 28: *High Stakes*, held on November 17, 2000, at the Trump Taj Majal in Atlantic City, he would fight Kevin Randleman, a wrestler who had been wreaking havoc in the Octagon since Couture had taken his leave. "I always thought fighting another wrestler would probably be the toughest fight for me because we come from similar backgrounds," said Couture. "I knew Randleman was potentially going to put me on the ground, put me on the bottom. Fortunately, I had analyzed my fight style when I took the time out. He took me down in the first two rounds. I was able to control him and keep him from damaging me, and then when I finally got a chance to tie him up and take him down in the third round, he hadn't been on his back at all. Basically he did the dying cockroach and didn't really know what to do with his legs or his hips or anything, and it allowed me to land some elbows and pretty hard shots to his face."

Couture's preparation had worked flawlessly, and as a result, he was awarded the UFC heavyweight championship belt once again. "That was my finest hour in MMA competition," said Couture. "I came back and actually set the goal of becoming the world champion again. It kind of happened the first time by accident; I really didn't set out to do it. It kind of fell in place and occurred, so I never really thought about it. After taking time off and concentrating on wrestling, I really set out to get that belt. I just knew when I finished wrestling that I had more work to do in the Octagon, and so to actually get in there and accomplish it was rewarding."

But in the evolving MMA game, no fighter was ever complete. His next fight against Pedro Rizzo (in UFC 31), a striker well versed on the ground, gave him a stern wake-up call. Although Couture managed to take Rizzo down in the first two rounds and to deliver the beating of his life, Rizzo weathered the abuse and got right back to his feet in the third round, ready to go toe-to-toe. "It was my toughest fight," said Couture. "I think all the guys I have fought have been tough. I think they were all great opponents. But Rizzo was certainly the toughest fight I had ever been in. I had to really suck it up to find a way to even finish that fight. That, more than anything, was contributed to Pedro. He withstood a whole barrage of punishment in the first round, and then he was able to come back in the second round and hang in there until the end of a highly energetic fight."

Couture had been pushed to his absolute limits with Rizzo, one of the best strikers in the sport, but it didn't surprise him. "Things seem to go in cycles," said Couture. "For a long time in the early days, Brazilian Jiu-Jitsu was the thing, and everyone was working on their submission skills because guys like Royce had been so effective, even giving up large amounts of weight. Nobody really knew what the submission game was all about. But now with all the cross-training taking place, guys are really, really hard to submit. They don't make the same mistakes as the early fighters in the UFC. They understand the game and know what is going on. That brought wrestlers into the sport, and they were able to take guys down and hold them down. For a stretch, they were the dominant force, and that caused people to analyze that, learn to sprawl and learn to defend the takedown. You began to see guys like Pedro Rizzo who are great strikers and very hard to take down. You can't put him down on the ground where you're most comfortable, and you have to stand up with the guy. That has brought striking back to the forefront of the sport. So now you have to be a well-rounded fighter—you have to be able to do everything, or someone is going to point it out to you in a way that hurts."

Couture received a unanimous decision from the judges in his back-and-forth battle with Rizzo, but the win came at a price—his leg was so beat up from kicks that he could hardly walk back to his hotel room. Couture decided to start over after he had realized that relying primarily on wrestling skills would no longer be acceptable in an evolving sport. To improve on his striking, he went to one of his former victims. "I think going to train with Maurice Smith just fixed a few things," said Couture. "After my first fight with Pedro, I fixed my stance, fixed my ability to maintain proper distance and control so I could check and throw punches. Working with Maurice allowed me to be a lot more patient."

To the surprise of most, Randy Couture trades punches with Chuck Liddell.

After taking Chuck Liddell to the mat, Randy Couture climbs into the mount and ends the fight with hammering fists.

That patience and practice proved invaluable in Couture's rematch with Rizzo in UFC 34, held on November 2, 2001. Instead of rushing in and trying to take Rizzo to the mat, Couture sat back and patiently waited. "Pedro is a real good counterpuncher and kicker. He kind of waits, tries to catch you coming in," said Couture. "I think the fact that I sat back and maintained my distance forced him to step out and be more aggressive. It kind of threw him off. He didn't really want to be aggressive; he was hoping that I was going to carry the fight to him, and he could catch me and pick me apart coming in. That didn't happen. I picked my shots, and picked the opportunity to close the distance and take him down. I think that game plan worked a lot better than the first time." In the third round, Couture trapped Rizzo against the fence and unleashed a flurry of punches, opening up a deep cut on Rizzo's face and spilling blood. The referee acted accordingly and pulled the fighters apart.

Couture had won his rematch with Rizzo by flawlessly setting up his shots and then executing classic ground and pound technique. He had proven, once again, why he was the king of the heavyweight mountain. But with other competitors in his division learning from his victories, Couture soon found himself up against an opponent who had copied his technique and strategy. This might not have been a problem if Couture was the heaviest fighter in his weight class, but with his body refusing to get over 235 pounds, Couture found himself at a serious disadvantage stepping into the Octagon with an opponent who was thirty pounds heavier.

When Couture took on Josh Barnett in UFC 36, he learned the hard way that a few extra pounds could help an opponent who was also skilled in the art of wrestling. Shortly into the bout, Cou-ture found himself pinned on the ground and trapped against the fence, absorbing an assault of downward strikes. Barnett beat on him with everything but the kitchen sink, and then he walked home with Couture's title belt. Many people credited Barnett's victory with the controlled substances he tested positive for after the bout. Barnett was stripped of his title but it was not given back to Couture. If he wanted to wear the heavyweight title belt once again, he would have to step into the Octagon.

Couture jumped right back into the mix to reclaim his belt by taking on Ricco Rodriguez in UFC 39: *The Warriors Return*, held on September 27, 2002, at the Mohegan Sun Arena. "For the first three rounds I was doing all the things that I wanted to do," said Couture. "I didn't concede those early takedowns, because I didn't want to be underneath the bigger guy. But giving up thirty pounds to a guy who knew how to use his weight and fight pretty well was a big difference. In later rounds, it basically started to wear me down."

Once again finding himself on the bottom, trapped under a larger opponent who pounded away with downward strikes, Couture struggled to regain his footing. In the process, however, he received one of the most serious injuries of his career. "It was an elbow. It just so happened that the point of Ricco's elbow went right in my eye socket," said Couture. "It blew out the very thin bone that separates your eye socket from your nasal passages. When it fractured, it trapped the muscles inside of my eye, so my eye wouldn't function properly. It was kind of like being in the Riddler's clubhouse; everything was slanted. I couldn't see and I knew something was wrong, and so I said I'd had enough. It was about six months trying to come back from that, and I actually still have a little bit of double vision in the lower part of my periphery vision."

Couture had suffered his second loss in a row. With his body still refusing to gain weight, he was no longer able to fend off the heavier opponents who were skilled in MMA competition. He was also thirty-eight years old, fifteen years past his prime. Although many people thought he had achieved all he could in the sport, Couture didn't agree. In his mind, he had never considered himself the strongest, fastest, or most gifted competitor to step into the Octagon, but through hard work he had always been able to focus and accomplish what he wanted to do. It was this at-

titude that allowed him to win fights—which gave him the ability to stay calm and relaxed and focus on this game plan. That trait didn't wither with age—it only grew stronger. "I think the biggest thing, looking at my career as a wrestler, is that I have the determination and will to succeed. It applies to anything in life. There were several times in my career where in big matches I came out on the short end. I lost in the Olympic trials four different times. I could have been very upset. I was upset that I lost, but I could have quit. I could have given up and said I was going to do something else. But because I had the attitude that I wasn't going to let that get me down

Randy Couture struggles to tie up with Tito Ortiz.

and that I was going to come back and do better, I had several other opportunities. I went on to win the National Championships. And so I just think that determination, and a deep-seated desire to continue to progress and learn, came from the sport of wrestling."

Instead of giving up, Couture analyzed his fight with Rodriguez to see how he could improve. He realized that while trapped on the bottom, he had been using his arms to control his opponent and create space. This might have worked with an opponent his size, but trying such a tactic with Rodriguez had worn him down. So in training he began using his legs to control an opponent on the ground instead of his arms, and it allowed him to conserve precious energy. He knew that this would help, but it still wouldn't give him the edge he needed to remain in the heavyweight division. To deal with this blockade, he decided to drop down to the light heavyweights. As it turned out, losing the weight proved less difficult than he'd thought. "I dropped right down to 215 about six weeks before my fight," said Couture. "I used to wrestle at 190 in college and internationally, so I had developed a system of cutting weight. I knew my body pretty well and it was like putting on an old shoe. I started running a little more and

Randy Couture snatches Tito Ortiz's leg to bring him to the ground.

Randy Couture takes Tito Ortiz's back and then works to apply a rear naked choke.

working out, and the weight came off real easy."

Dropping the weight was one thing—competing in the light heavyweights, arguably the most competitive division in the UFC, was another. Many people thought he should have a few warm-up fights to see how he handled the weight loss, but just as in the past, Couture stepped into the Octagon to battle for a championship belt immediately.

Although Tito Ortiz was the current light heavyweight champion, Couture would not be fighting him for the title belt—he would be fighting Chuck Liddell, a striker who had racked up a brutal string of knockouts in the Octagon. For two years, Liddell had been after Ortiz, and for two years Ortiz had ducked him. The UFC promoters were at a loss as to how to handle the sit-

uation, until Couture entered the division. They decided to have Liddell face Couture, and the winner of the bout would be awarded the interim title belt. If Ortiz wanted to prove he was the undisputed champion, he had to step up and face the winner. "I thought it was a really good opportunity for me," said Couture. "I was kind of stuck between weight classes, with the trend in the heavyweight division being the larger guys who not only are big but also know how to fight. I felt like I should go down to the light heavyweights and compete against guys who are a lot closer to my size. So I felt real fortunate to move right into a title contention situation right away."

To prepare for Liddell, Couture studied videotapes of his opponent's previous fights, developed a game plan, and wrote down everything on a calendar that he planned to accomplish up until the fight. Then he jumped into lifting weights, running, and sparring hours each day with fellow UFC competitors Matt Lindland, Dan Henderson, and Evan Tanner. He brought in a host of boxers who could teach him how to throw proper punches and land combinations. To maintain the best possible physical condition at this lower weight, he made modifications to his diet. "I cut out all the dairy—or as much of the dairy as I possibly could. I tried to increase the amount of raw vegetables in my diet. I tried to separate my carbohydrate meals from my protein meals, and I added a supplement called Light Force, which is basically just a big variety of greens in powder form. And then I kept drink-

ing water throughout the day. All of this was designed to try to alkalize my system from all the stress that builds up from training, which allowed my muscles to stay more oxygenated. That, in turn, allowed me to train harder."

Arriving at the arena in Las Vegas on the night of June 6, 2003, for UFC 43: *Meltdown*, Couture felt in the best shape of his life. Backstage he began his warm-up routine with stretching and light sparring. When his muscles were loose, he tossed on the gloves and began fairly intense sparring with a teammate, executing the moves that were in his game plan. As he did this, he thought about the fight ahead. "It's the one-on-one nature of the sport that I love," said Couture. "That is what I loved about wrestling as well.

Randy Couture keeps Tito Ortiz pinned down.

You have friends and people around you who make you better, but when it comes down to it, it is about you going out there and showing what you are capable of."

Being that this was one of the most anticipated matches the UFC had seen in a long time, both fighters were given lavish introductions as they made their way toward the Octagon. Once they touched gloves in the center of the ring, however, it was all business. Immediately Liddell came forward, jabbing from a distance and trying to find a weakness in Couture's defense. As Liddell's reaching punches slowly drew nearer, Couture made his move, running forward to tie up in the clinch. Liddell shuffled furiously back-

wards, throwing wild strikes in an attempt to keep Couture off him, but just as he was beginning to escape, Couture threw an upward knee that caught Liddell right in the face. It wasn't a knockout shot, but it was enough to make Liddell concerned about Couture's striking ability. "The game plan was to hunt Chuck down," said Couture. "I watched seven or eight of his fights on tape, and every single guy gave him too much space, too much respect. He had earned that respect through all the guys whom he knocked out, but they had played right into his game. They allowed him to control the tempo, and land what he wanted to land. So I kind of decided to get close to him. Maybe I would get knocked out,

Mounted on top of Tito Ortiz, Randy Couture blasts his opponent with punches. "I said all along that it would come down to who got the takedown and established the top position," says Couture, "and that was me."

but I was going to get into his space and try to stay there. Fortunately for me, it worked out. It really threw him off the fight."

They began to circle one another, Liddell trying to find an opening, but all the while Couture came forward. To keep Couture off him, Liddell threw a kick to the leg, and that's when Couture shot in, hoisted Liddell high off his feet and then slammed him down to the canvas. "To get a striker down, you basically have two options," said Couture. "Either you go on the offense, throwing punches and attacking them, which causes them to cover and stop moving their feet, and from there you can then finish with a takedown. Or you wait, try to control the range, basically bait them into punching and kicking you. When they're posted on one leg, or extended for that punch, then you can slip underneath and penetrate for the takedown."

When Liddell escaped back to his feet, Couture continued to press the fight, and he began to take his opponent down at will. But what truly came as a surprise was how he outboxed his opponent in between takedowns. Every time Liddell threw his looping punches, Couture would slip them and then fire rights and lefts straight down the middle. He dominated on both the ground and his feet, and in the third round, he ended the fight by hovering over his downed foe and landing a barrage of unanswered punches.

Couture had done what few thought he could do at the age of thirty-nine—absolutely devastate the most feared striker in the UFC. Once again he had a title belt wrapped around his waist, but to truly be considered the champion, he would have to beat Ortiz, a man known for putting the best wrestlers on their backs and beating them into submission.

"My focus was different while preparing for Tito. I worked a lot of footwork and striking getting ready for Chuck, and I worked a lot of being on the bottom for Tito," said Couture. "I needed to be ready for the possibility that he was going to take me down and try to hold me down. That's how he won, without exception, almost every fight he has been in. He would take guys down and control them, dominate from the top. So I figured not too much was going to change; that's what he needed to do if he was going to win. I already felt like I had years of experience taking guys down, and so I didn't really need to train that hard for that. But getting up off the bottom, creating some ammo so I would be difficult to take down in the fighting situation, is what I focused on mainly."

Couture's training proved beneficial when face-to-face with the "Huntington Beach Bad Boy" in UFC 44: *Undisputed*, held on September 26, 2003, in Las Vegas. At the beginning of the fight, Ortiz tried everything he could think of to bring Couture down, but the wrestler refused to budge. After a brief power struggle, Couture began taking Ortiz down, trapping him against the fence, and then beating him with punches and elbows. It was the very tactic Ortiz had been using on his opponents for years, and just like all his previous victims, he was not able to escape the relentless punishment.

Other than a few submission attempts by Ortiz, Couture dominated the entire five rounds, and when the bout fell into the hands of the judges, little doubt existed in the minds of the spectators who had won. "It went exactly as I had planned," said Couture. "I said all along that it would come down to who got the takedown and established the top position, and that was me."

At thirty-nine years old, Couture had completely destroyed the most popular and well-rounded fighter in the light heavy-weight division. Nevertheless, maintaining a game plan that works doesn't mean Couture hasn't worked on improving his skills. Every day in practice he continued to drill submissions. "I like arm triangles—I seem to find myself in that position a lot. I'm trying to get better at leg locks, heel hooks and ankle locks," said Couture. "I'm trying to focus on that a lot right now. I know a lot of submissions, but knowing them and having the ability to apply them in real time, in just a few seconds, is the biggest difference. With a lot of the submissions, if you don't get them you can cost yourself position, and a lot of time losing position may cost you the fight. That is something you have to weigh out."

Despite fighting in the most aggressive form of hand-to-hand combat on earth, Couture feels he is a simple guy living a normal lifestyle, and he is almost hesitant to acknowledge the fact that through his sportsmanship, courage, and drive to win, he has become a hero to thousands. Along with inspiring many athletes in their thirties to realize that they shouldn't consider themselves over the hill, he has also inspired thousands of wrestlers to begin competing in MMA competition, ensuring that the sport will continue to evolve. To these young hopefuls,

A grieving Tito Ortiz shows his respect as he hands the light heavyweight title belt over to Randy Couture.

Couture has this advice: "First of all, you need to keep an open mind and to check your ego at the door. Then you have to go out and find an environment where there are guys who have the other skills you need to learn, for both striking and submission. Wrestling is a great foundation, a great place to start, but you need to learn a lot more to be effective and last in this sport. Most of all you need to have a desire to compete. A true warrior is the guy who has the spirit to go out there and deal with the adversity of competition. It doesn't really matter what your skill level is, but rather that you have a willingness to go out there and compete."

King of the Slam

After throwing a flurry of powerful punches, Matt Hughes hefted Gil Castillo off his feet, power slammed him to the canvas, and then scooted him over to the fence to begin his demolition. He dropped elbows and punches to the body and face. He even stood up on occasion so he could dive forward with downward strikes. Castillo, who had been trained by the Gracie family, attempted one submission after another, but nothing could contain the ferocity Hughes had brought into the Octagon. Hughes was a wrestler on a mission, and while thrashing his opponent with dozens of strikes, he opened a bloody cut on Castillo's forehead with an inadvertent head butt. When Castillo told the doctor he was having trouble seeing, the fight was brought to a halt near the end of the first round. Just like Couture, Hughes had once again proved just how dominant a well-rounded wrestler could be in modern mixed martial arts (MMA) competition.

Matt Hughes' first MMA competition was in a small Chicago-based show in 1996. He didn't train for the fight, he had virtually no striking skills to speak of, and he felt, nonetheless, quite confident stepping into the cage with an experienced kickboxer named Craig "The Terminator" Quick. "As soon as he got close enough to kick me, I just shot in and took him down," said Hughes. "I instantly put my knee on his stomach and started pounding him. He gave up. The entire fight lasted thirty seconds. Now, I didn't know who Pat Miletich was, but he was actually refereeing the fight. People were telling me that he was the world champ, but I could have cared less about who the world champion was at the time."

Hughes had not entered the competition to make a name for himself or to find a camp of fighters to train with. He had entered for fun, and so when the event was over, he put the MMA competition behind him and headed back to his job as assistant wrestling coach of Eastern Illinois University. But it wasn't long before he once again thirsted for the thrill of competition. His first MMA bout had reminded him just how much he missed the rush of one-on-one combat that he'd experienced while wrestling in high school and college, and soon he found himself competing in another MMA bout, this time in Extreme Challenge 21, held on October 17, 1998.

Miletich was sitting on the sidelines, and he remembered the young wrestler from his debut. He pointed him out to his manager, Monte Cox, who was on the prowl for new talent. Together they watched Hughes put away his first opponent by taking him to the ground and pounding

After putting Gil Castillo on his back, Matt Hughes begins his assault.

him into submission with strikes, and then they watched him earn a unanimous decision over Dave Menne, an experienced competitor who would later become the middleweight champion of the UFC. Although Hughes tapped out in the finals when Dennis Hallman caught him in a guillotine choke, both Miletich and Cox sensed the young wrestler was a diamond in the rough.

When Hughes fought a month later in Chicago, Miletich and Cox were there, and they approached the young wrestler after the show. "I had heard about Pat Miletich at the time, and he came up to me and asked if I would think about coming to Iowa and training with him," said

Hughes. "I thought about it, and I didn't think it would be such a bad idea." Although Hughes wasn't quite sure if he wanted to give up his life for the sport, he concluded it couldn't hurt to travel to Iowa and just take a look.

On his first visit, Hughes rolled on the mats with both Miletich and Jeremy Horn, two experienced UFC competitors. By the time practice was over, he was hooked on their style of training. It wasn't that he dominated on the ground and liked the feeling of thrashing his sparring partners; it was the exact opposite. Training with Miletich and his crew made him realize just how much he had to learn, and that got his blood pumping.

Over the course of the next several years, Hughes traveled to Iowa once a month, and each time he picked up something new. "In wrestling you never want to go to your back—it's the worst place to be," said Hughes. "When you are training for MMA, you need to get comfortable on your back because chances are you will end up there at one time or another. Jeremy Horn started working with me on that, and I got over it. I actually became quite competitive there. But the boxing was something else."

Even though Hughes was right-handed, he had begun fighting in MMA competition as a southpaw because he had always wrestled with his right foot forward. "I went through a couple of fights that way, but I just didn't have the boxing skills that I needed because my strong hand was forward," said Hughes. "I had a really great jab, but I just couldn't do anything with my left hand because I didn't have any power in it. So Pat turned me around, but sometimes I still mix up my feet to set up the takedown. If I know I'm going to take someone down, I'll throw a double jab, a right hand, and then I'll step with my right foot—that way I'm back in my comfortable stance, with my right foot forward. So there are different tricks you can do. But being primarily a wrestler, I learned that I really needed to concentrate on becoming a better boxer, not a better wrestler."

As Gil Castillo tries to stand, Matt Hughes rips his legs out from underneath him.

Trapping Hayato Sakurai against the fence, Matt Hughes demonstrates classic ground and pound as he unleashed his rage with his elbows.

While honing his skills at the Miletich camp, Hughes realized that he could have a future in the sport. Few people in the gym could stop him from taking them down, and once they hit the mat he could apply any one of his newfound submissions. After making the monthly commute for almost a year, in 2000, Pat asked him to move to Iowa full time. "It was a very big decision, because it would mean leaving a lot behind," said Hughes. "But I think I made the right one by going to Pat and the UFC."

After dominating his opponents in numerous smaller competitions, Hughes made his Octagon debut at UFC 22, held on September 24, 1999. His opponent was Valeri Ignatov, a Bulgarian sambo champion who had won countless submission tournaments in Eastern Europe. When the two newcomers were announced, most people thought it would be a classic match between a wrestler and a submission expert. No one knew, however, just how much Hughes had learned while studying with Miletich. "He was the first

Matt Hughes drops an elbow to a defenseless Carlos Newton.

Matt Hughes tries to prevent Carlos Newton from passing his guard.

guy that I actually went after that I wanted to manage," said Cox. "I just thought he had a real good chance of being somebody. You show him a few things, and by the end of the day, he is using them on you. He was a really fast learner; he really wanted to learn. You could just tell that Matt Hughes had what it took right from the beginning. He is a super nice guy. He is a guy who just loves a challenge. If you tell him he can't do something, look out, because he'll do it. If you tell him that he can't learn to stand up and knock people out, watch out, because that is where he is headed. The guy is an absolute machine."

The spectators at UFC 22 witnessed this when in the opening seconds of the fight Hughes dropped low, scooped Ignatov off his feet, carried him a few seconds on his shoulder, and then turned his opponent upside down and dumped him on his head. A dazed Ignatov captured Hughes in his guard, but the wrestler wasn't through making an impact on his feet and stood back up. Hughes began landing shots, left and right, and after beating on his opponent with his fists, he began taking Ignatov down at will. When Hughes returned to his corner at the end of the first round, Miletich was there to coach him. "Pass his guard, get position first, and then destroy him. You're winning the fight, don't get crazy."

Hughes tried to stick to the game plan, but he liked the damage he was inflicting on his feet. At the beginning of the second round, he caught Ignatov with a hard left hand. Ignatov shook his head and then came right back, looking to trade punches, but he takes another hard left that backed him up. Ignatov was stubborn, and when

After seizing Matt Hughes's arm, Carlos Newton jumps into an arm bar.

Matt Hughes defends an arm bar by rolling.

Cupping the back of Carlos Newton's head, Matt Hughes brings up a powerful knee.

he came in for a third time, Hughes let his right hand fly, nearly knocking his opponent off his feet. Miletich shouted orders from the sidelines, and Hughes followed them immediately. He landed a knee to Ignatov's midsection and tore into him with punches. The bout went the distance, but there was no doubt in the judges' minds which fighter had dominated from start to finish.

After his victory, Hughes returned to Miletich Fighting Systems to further hone his skills. He had liked throwing punches, but knowing they weren't his strong suit, he armed himself with a few tricks. "If I'm going to fight a superior strik-er, I'm always looking for an advantage," said Hughes. "And my advantage would definitely not be on my feet, it will be on the ground. But before shooting in, I learned to throw my hands. When you throw a punch at someone, the natural reaction is to bring the hands up. It gets your opponent thinking that they need to defend themselves, and maybe they won't be throwing knees. So you throw two or three jabs to get their hands up, and then it is a lot safer to go in and take a shot."

When Hughes defeated Marcelo Aguiar in UFC 26: *Ultimate Field of Dreams*, on June 9, 2000, it became clear to everyone that he had what it

Matt Hughes throws a huge right cross at Sean Sherk.

While attempting to take Sean Sherk to the ground, Matt Hughes is caught in a guillotine choke.

Matt Hughes throws a knee to the face of Sean Sherk.

took to get to the top of the welterweight division. That posed a problem because the current UFC welterweight titleholder was his trainer, Miletich. The two would never fight each other, and so Hughes stepped down from the UFC to allow Miletich his time in the sun. He turned all his focus onto training. "I'd wake up in the morning and go for a run, and then come back and eat breakfast," said Hughes. "I basically followed a weightlifter's diet—that's about six small meals a day. The only fats I took in were through nuts, and I stayed away from the simple sugars. In the afternoon I lifted weights, then did some light pad work or grappling. Then in the evening it was hard training. It was hard pads on Monday. Tuesday it would be hard grappling. Wednesday it would be hard sparring. Thursday

it was hard grappling again. In the afternoons of those days, sometimes I would run stadiums carrying one of my training partners on my back. Then we'd do sprints or run up a quarter-mile hill eight times in a row."

In less than a year, Hughes was a completely different person than when he first walked into Miletich Fighting Systems. "I had learned to relax," said Hughes. "I was a better all-around fighter as far as grappling, setting up my shots with strikes to get people on the ground. And my striking had come a long way as well. So I was a well-rounded person, as opposed to when I walked in there. Right before I went to Miletich, I was just an animal in the cage. Nobody could match my power and the intensity that I had. But that got me into trouble—I'd get caught in sub-

While trying to take Matt Hughes to the mat, Sean Sherk takes a knee to the face.

Comfortable fighting from his back, Matt Hughes attempts a leg lock on Frank Trigg.

mission holds. So I would just pick my opponents up and slam them down. Unfortunately, that doesn't work all the time. So Pat made me more methodical. Instead of going out there and being an animal, it was a chess match. I was a good enough chess player, so to speak, that I could win my matches."

He got a chance to see just how well he could play chess when Miletich lost his title belt to Carlos Newton in UFC 31. After Hughes had waited patiently for many months, he wasted no time climbing back into the Octagon to get some redemption for his trainer.

In the locker room of the MGM Grand Garden

Arena in Las Vegas, Nevada, on the night of November 2, 2001, Hughes prepared for the toughest match of his life. "I like to have a good sweat going," said Hughes. "That keeps a good submission artist like Carlos Newton from applying any quick submissions on a dry body. Then I shadow box, pummel a little bit. I don't slap my face or anything like that. I just go in there like it's a job. I don't see fighting as confrontation. I see it as my job right now. The reason I'm in the sport is because I happen to be good at it, and it comes naturally to me. If I wasn't any good at it, I wouldn't be in the sport. I'm smart enough to know that I can do things with my body besides

With his arm wrapped tightly around Frank Trigg's throat, Matt Hughes wins the bout with a rear naked choke.

Matt Hughes with the UFC welterweight title belt.

knocked them back one by one. He defeated Hayato Sakurai with strikes in UFC 36: *Worlds Collide*, on March 22, 2002. He defeated Newton once again in UFC 38: *The Brawl at Royal Albert Hall*, on July 13, 2002. Then it was the destruction of Gil Castillo in UFC 40 on November 22, 2002, Sean Sherk in UFC 42: *Sudden Impact*, on April 25, 2003, and Frank Trigg in UFC 45: *Revolution*, on November 21, 2003. There was no doubt about it—Hughes was the most successful champion in the greatest MMA event on earth.

Hughes' dominance in the Octagon not only inspired millions of fight fans, but it also encouraged even more wrestlers searching for a way to make a living to begin MMA competition. "Coming in with a good wrestling background, these guys are going to know how to get their bodies in shape," said Hughes. "But they really have to push themselves. In the morning they are going to have to wake up and go for a run. Come back and eat breakfast. They need to lift weights sometime during the day, whether it is in the morning or the evening. And they need to work on their boxing and their submissions. They will have to get well rounded, because that is the key in the fight game today—to be well rounded. The day where the Gracies were dominant on the ground is over. So they need to be well rounded, work on all aspects of the fight game. Being a wrestler is the best thing to walk into MMA with, because you can learn everything else easy. If you take a boxer and try to teach him wrestling, it takes forever. If you take a Brazilian Jiu-Jitsu artist and try to teach him wrestling, it takes forever. Wrestling is something you cannot pick up in a year. It just takes so much time. I would say these wrestlers are at an advantage coming into the sport—they just need to work on the other things."

getting my head knocked in all the time. So the reason I'm here is because I'm good at it and because I love to compete."

He took this attitude into the Octagon with Newton, and when he found himself caught in a triangle choke in the second round, he picked Newton up, he carried him over to the fence on his shoulders, and then, just as he was losing consciousness from the chokehold, he slammed Newton to the mat, knocking him unconscious. Although they were both incoherent, Hughes was given the win and the welterweight title belt. As others climbed up to steal it from him, he

The Law

Matt Lindland had been waiting for this night for almost six months—a chance to get revenge on Falaniko Vitale. At UFC 43: Meltdown, held on June 6, 2003, in Las Vegas, Nevada, Lindland had taken Vitale's back less than two minutes into the bout, and then he arched his weight back to slam his opponent head first onto the canvas. Lindland had performed thousands of similar throws during his wrestling career, but this time he didn't receive the same positive result. When their bodies came down, Lindland's head struck the canvas, knocking him unconscious.

Lindland didn't waste time sulking about the loss. He had jumped right back into training, preparing for the rematch at UFC 45, on November 21, 2003. Vitale had boasted that he'd won their first bout because he'd felt the throw coming and shifted his weight to throw Lindland off, so when Lindland faced him for the second time, he planned to show the young fighter just what a true wrestler was made of. In the first round, Lindland took his opponent to the mat and dominated from the top position. In the second round, he trapped Vitale against the fence and landed shots to the body and face. In the third round, he pinned one of his opponent's arms to the mat and pounded away with punches, forcing Vitale to tap in submission. Dominating the bout from start to finish, he reminded everyone why he was the number-one-ranked middleweight fighter in the UFC.

Matt Lindland had never paid much attention to mixed martial arts (MMA) competition until he saw Randy Couture, an old college wrestling buddy, kick ass in the UFC in 1997. Lindland thought to himself: "Hell, I'm a whole lot tougher than that guy, and he's winning all his fights. I might as well get into this." To decide on how to get involved in promotions, he stopped by to see Couture, who happened to live close by in Lindland's hometown of Linwood, Oregon. He got some names and numbers of the smaller promotions and then began to place some calls. With his more than impressive amateur wrestling accomplishments, which included being a five-time National Champion and a three-time Pan-Am Champion, he quickly secured a slot in an event called the World Fighting Federation.

On February 14, 1997, Lindland flew to Birmingham, Alabama, to compete in his first MMA competition. In preparation for the bout, he hadn't thrown a single punch or kick. He hadn't learned how to defend against the more popular submission holds. Even though he understood that the only rules in his match would be no biting or gouging, the only thing he had done in preparation was to roll around on the mats. Truthfully, he wasn't taking the whole thing very seriously. It was just something he was doing for fun. "It was great," said Lindland. "I just showed up and fought. I took my opponent down and started beating on him. They stopped the fight early because I was completely dominating. They called it a TKO, but my opponent said the ref shouldn't have stopped it. Since I was really enjoying what I was doing, I asked the ref if we could fight again. He allowed it, so I took my opponent down, beat on him some more, and the ref stopped it again."

Lindland liked the way his first match had gone, and so he decided to enter another small promotion just a few months later. Still he didn't bother to learn how to strike or avoid submis-

sions, and yet the damage he inflicted in the ring this time was even more brutal than in his first bout. Instead of just grounding his opponent and beating him with his fists, Lindland got creative and started dropping elbows and knees.

After these two impressive wins in MMA competition, promoters began calling him to compete, but Lindland turned them all down. As much as he would have liked to continue in the sport, he had a lifelong goal to achieve. The 2000 Olympic Games in Sydney, Australia, were less than three years away, and if he planned to bring home a medal, he would have to abandon all his hobbies and focus exclusively on wrestling.

For two solid years he hit the mats, honing his skills to compete with the world's top wrestlers. Making it on the Olympic team, however, proved to be rather difficult. In the U.S. trials, he lost to Keith Sieracki, which meant that he wouldn't be

Matt Lindland throws Ricardo Almeida. As the two come down, Matt Lindland's head hits the canvas, and he is knocked unconscious.

While closing the gap, Matt Lindland is hit by Phil Baroni.

heading to Sydney. Lindland had been wrestling since he was a child and he knew how to handle loss, but in this case he felt he had won the match, so he brought the matter to court. Several months later, he emerged from a mountain of legal papers and the courtroom with two things: the nickname 'The Law,' and an overturned loss in his match with Sieracki. He was heading to the Olympics after all.

When the moment he had been waiting a lifetime for finally arrived in summer 2000, Lindland performed like a true champion and took home a silver medal. It was the greatest moment in his life, one worth relishing. But like most wrestlers, Lindland couldn't stay inactive for long. He had been following MMA competition for the past several years, and although he realized that the competitors were only getting tougher, he still felt he could dominate with his wrestling skills, even at the highest level of the sport. After he returned to Oregon, one of the first things he did was call the UFC. With a silver medal strapped around his neck, he didn't have to do much convincing to get in.

Lindland made his UFC debut only a few months later in Tokyo, Japan. As he stepped into the Octagon on the night of December 16, 2000, for UFC 29: *Defense of the Belts*, the commentators pumped up his recent accomplishment in Sydney, but they also proposed doubt. His opponent, Yoji Anjo, had once gone toe-to-toe with the infamous Tank Abbott, and although he had come out on the losing end of the exchange, he had proven that he could strike. If Lindland couldn't

Matt Lindland struggles
to bring Phil Baroni to
the ground.

take him down, they suspected that he would be in trouble.

As it turned out, Lindland didn't have to worry about trading punches in order to bring his opponent to the ground. Only a few seconds into the bout, it was Anjo who shot in. Lindland defended the takedown with the sprawl, and with Anjo trapped on all fours, Lindland delivered a series of knees to the top of his opponent's head. When Anjo went to his back, Lindland crawled into the mount and delivered a host of elbows to the temple and punches to the face. Anjo flailed and jerked from side to side, but Lindland understood too much about positioning to let him get away. Three minutes into the bout, the referee saw that Anjo had taken enough abuse, and he pulled Lindland off him.

Beating a downed opponent into submission

had once again proven to be an effective strategy, and so Lindland decided to keep it. He dispensed with his next opponent, Ricardo Almeida, in much the same way in UFC 31. But Lindland didn't want to be just a one-dimensional fighter. He wanted to be able to get out there and compete with the best of them, and so he went to train with Maurice Smith to learn the proper way to punch and kick. He then took that knowledge back to Couture, with whom he had begun training full time. "There are so many different drills that we do," said Lindland. "From stand-up punching drills to kickboxing drills. I already know how to take a guy down, bring him out of his element by placing him on the ground. But more importantly, I want to learn how to get in there and strike with those guys. I've only been doing this for a short amount of time, so my striking is still my weakness, but I'm working to finish

some fights while standing up because I like that kind of work. I have fun doing it. That, I think, is my biggest strength, liking my job. My other biggest strength is the ability to get in there and compete. Being mentally tough isn't something you're born with, and I think wrestling is something that allows you to develop that."

Lindland's mental toughness and his striking skills would both be put to the test in UFC 34, held on November 2, 2001. His opponent, Phil Baroni, had been given the nickname "The New York Bad Ass" for a reason—he liked to go in slugging and not stop until his opponent was knocked out. "I had only seen him fight one time, and all he did was take his opponent down and ground and pound him," said Lindland. "I was just starting to work on developing some of my kicks, but they really weren't that good or effective. I don't think I had much of a game plan.

Matt Lindland shooting in to take Ivan Salaverry to the ground.

Atlantic City. This time, however, Lindland would dominate the majority of the fight. "I knew how to prepare for him the second time," said Lindland. "Circle, stay away from his strikes, take him down, control him on the ground, and then finish him with ground and pound." Although Lindland didn't manage the finishing part of his game plan, he executed all the rest and received a unanimous decision as a result.

Even though Lindland has proven repeatedly that a successful amateur wrestler can still dominate in the Octagon with only limited strikes and submissions, he continues to improve on his game. "Fighting is a way of life for me now. I never stop training," said Lindland. "I train like an MMA fighter now. Although I haven't got any submissions in the ring, I'm working on it. But even more importantly, I have a willingness to get out there and compete against anybody. There are a lot of fighters out there now who want to pick their opponents. They always want to know what the other guy's record is. Whom did he beat? I think you can't give a damn what his record is or who he has beaten—you just have to go out there and fight him. That exemplifies a warrior."

SECTION THREE

The Strikers

Time to Brawl

On September 9, 1994, at UFC 3, Keith Hackney stepped into the Octagon to face Emmanuel Yarborough, an accomplished sumo wrestler who stood six feet eight inches tall and weighed 620 pounds. Hackney had no idea how he could hurt a man that size, but knowing that this was his one chance to prove that grapplers didn't own the world, he cast all fear aside. In the opening seconds of the bout, he approached his massive foe and arched an open palm over his shoulder with all his might. "I buried my hand in his face, and he went down," said Hackney. "Unfortunately, he got back up."

With the giant lumbering toward him once again, Hackney began throwing leg kicks. When the angered beast caught one in his swollen hands, Hackney bounced on one foot and landed a series of uppercuts that toppled his opponent for the second time. With Yarborough on all fours, Hackney came around from the rear and hammered away on the opponent's massive head with his fists. Taking unfamiliar abuse, the largest man ever to step foot into the Octagon found himself at a striker's mercy, and he tapped in submission. Hackney found the victory gratifying, but his work in the Octagon would not be complete until he taught a similar lesson to a stealthy Brazilian named Royce Gracie.

Although Royce Gracie swept the first two UFC events, quickly submitting every boxer, karate practitioner, and kickboxer who stepped into the Octagon with him, there were still millions of martial artists around the world who refused to acknowledge that if they didn't know how to fight on the ground they would be quickly submitted by a grappler. One such striker was Keith Hackney.

Growing up in a Chicago suburb riddled with gangs, Hackney had studied everything from Tang Soo Do to boxing in order to protect himself. He had been in his share of street fights, in which the hardest hitter usually won. So when Hackney saw the first UFC, he found it hard to believe that a 178-pound Brazilian who spent the majority of his time on his back could actually defeat an experienced striker. Hackney felt that with his arsenal of punches and kicks he could fend off Gracie and knock him out. The only way to be sure, however, was to climb into the Octagon himself. "There was just never anything like the UFC," said Hackney. "I mean, how do you really ever know what you are learning actually works. The UFC was basically the only proving ground for all the training you ever did in your

With Emmanuel Yarborough gripping his leg, Keith Hackney throws punches to the face, dropping his 620-pound opponent. "I didn't care if he picked me up, slammed me, and broke my neck," says Hackney. "I didn't care if he broke my leg, anything else. I went out there basically to give Manny the fight of his life."

life, and it was against someone who is just as skilled as you are, in an environment where anything goes."

Immediately, Hackney filled out the application in the back of *Black Belt Magazine* and sent it to the UFC. "I started training my ass off, and then they sent me a letter saying that the fight card was filled for the next event but that they might use me at a later date," said Hackney. "Back then, they only held one event a year, and I thought, 'Yeah right, it's fixed.' I thought I would never hear from them again."

Hackney cut back on his training and buried himself in work. Then, on September 6, 1994, only four days before UFC 3, Hackney received a telephone call from the UFC asking if he wanted to fight. "They told me that Ken Shamrock and

Royce Gracie would be competing in the tournament," said Hackney, "but that my first bout would be against a six-hundred pound sumo guy." I said, "It doesn't really matter. If I am going to fight to win, I'm going to have to fight everyone anyway. If you guys want me down there, I'm in."

Hackney flew to Charlotte, North Carolina, two days later, and after he had defeated an opponent who was four feet wide and three feet thick, he deservedly earned the nickname "The Giant Killer." Despite breaking several bones in his hand and being unable to continue in the tournament, Hackney became an inspiration and hope for traditional martial artists around the world. As far as they were concerned, Sumo was a grappling art and Hackney felled the largest,

As Robbie Lawler throws his powerful right hook, Aaron Riley delivers a knee to his opponent's midsection.

strongest grappler around. Many people thought Hackney would be the one to finally stop Gracie in his tracks. Hackney felt likewise; so after he recovered from his broken hand, he entered the Octagon with Gracie in UFC 4, held on December 16, 1994, and he advanced on his Brazilian opponent with the intention of beating him with strikes until he was knocked unconscious.

Robbie Lawler goes in for the kill after knocking Tiki Ghosn to the canvas with a bashing forearm.

Tank Abbott charges forward with punches, looking to knock out submission expert Frank Mir.

His game plan worked quite well in the beginning. When Gracie shot for his legs, Hackney countered with the sprawl and then used the opportunity to land three powerful uppercuts. Only a few seconds later, Gracie delivered again, and this time Hackney sprawled and backed away. When Gracie managed to corner him against the fence and close the gap, Hackney seized Gracie's gi (uniform) with his left hand and began throwing punches with his right.

It looked as if Hackney might succeed with his mission until Gracie pulled him down into his guard. Fueled by adrenaline, Hackney managed to break free of a chokehold, even land a punch to Gracie's face, but instead of backing out and forcing his opponent up to his feet, Hackney decided to throw another punch. Gracie parried the shot, pulled Hackney back down into his embrace, and then locked him in an arm bar that forced Hackney to tap the canvas in submission.

The loss was tough for Hackney to accept, but instead of making up excuses, he took it as a learning experience. Just like dozens of strikers in the first few UFCs, he now understood that if

Out of his element on the ground, Thai Boxer Duane Ludwig tries to defend himself against Genki Sudo.

Gripping Genki Sudo's leg, Duane Ludwig fires away with downward punches.

Cupping the back of Sean Alvarez's face, Wesley Correira brings up a knee to his opponent's jaw.

he didn't know how to grapple or to at least defend the takedown, he was little more than a fish out of water. "You talk to people today, and they say how the fighters have gotten much better. Well, you know what, the only reason they have gotten much better is because of how everything started and people who found out what works and what doesn't work," said Hackney. "A lot of people talk to me today and they think I'm still fighting the way I was in 1993. Now I do everything: ground, takedowns, countering take-

downs. I've just really matured as a fighter because of the UFC."

With traditional martial artists such as Hackney relearning the fighting arts, it would be some time before they would find success against the grapplers and wrestlers in the UFC. However, a few strikers already had a head start, and they managed to put up a struggle against the early ground fighters who were running the show. The first was David "Tank" Abbott. Although he was introduced as a street brawler in his Octagon

While trading blows, Wesley Correira lands a perfect right hand to the jaw of Sean Alvarez.

debut on July 14, 1995, in UFC 6, he had been boxing for thirteen years and wrestling since the age of nine. "The UFC wanted to make an example out of me," said Abbott. "They wanted to show how their martial artists could beat up the big, bad street fighter. They called me Tank, because they wanted me to be a real life version of Tank Murdoch, the street fighter in the movie *Every Which Way But Loose*. I saw all these guys fighting in the UFC, and I thought, 'These guys right here don't know how to fight.' They go to a dojo, and they think they know how to fight? I'd been fighting in the streets all my life. It's differ-

ent than going to a karate dojo and pretend fighting. You're actually fighting for your life. There are no rules, and anything can happen. So I went in there and said, 'Listen, I'll show you mothers how to fight.' No one knew that I had been wrestling longer than most of the guys in there, and I had probably boxed longer than them as well. They all focused on me being a street fighter. Well, it blew up in their faces."

In his first bout in UFC 6, on the night of July 14, 1995, Abbott took on John Matua, who claimed he had studied the Hawaiian art of bone-breaking. After he had knocked Matua off bal-

Both Pete Spratt (right) and Robbie Lawler (left) land kicks.

Vitor Belfort lands a powerful knee to the face of Marvin Eastman.

Pulling down Edwin Dewees' head, Rich Franklin brings up a knee.

ance with a wild right, Abbott chased his opponent's face clear across the Octagon. Although most of his shots missed their target by mere inches, two powerful punches collided with Matua's face, turning his legs to rubber. The Hawaiian hit the floor, unconscious, but Abbott didn't stop there. He dropped all his weight down onto his opponent, and bashed his head with a powerful forearm. The entire bout had lasted eighteen seconds.

Even though Abbott managed to rack up a string of impressive knockouts over the next several years, when he found himself against ground specialists such as Dan Severn or Oleg Tackarov, he just couldn't bring enough to the table to pull out a victory.

It wasn't until Marco Ruas entered the picture in UFC 7, held on September 8, 1995, that a striker managed to carry home the title belt, but as people shortly learned, he wasn't just a striker.

Pedro Rizzo chops away at Ricco Rodriguez's legs.

For the past fifteen years Ruas had understood the importance of cross-training, and he had studied both grappling and wrestling. In his quarterfinal bout against Larry Cureton in UFC 7, Ruas demonstrated his submission skills by taking his opponent to the mat and forcing him to tap out with a heel hook. In his semifinal bout, he took on expert grappler Remco Pardoel. Finding his much larger opponent mounted on top of him shortly into the fight, Ruas demon-strated his wrestling ability as he reversed his opponent, climbed into the mount himself, and then rained down punches that ended the fight. And in the finals against Paul "The Polar Bear" Varelans, who stood six feet eight inches tall and weighed over three hundred pounds, Ruas showed his striking ability by keeping his distance and landing repeated kicks to his opponent's legs that eventually toppled the giant.

Many fans thought Ruas represented the new

authority in the Octagon, a striker who could counter everything the grapplers and wrestlers could throw at him and then slowly wear them down with punches and kicks. But after losing a decision to Taktarov in Ultimate Ultimate '95, Ruas disappeared from the ranks of the UFC. It wasn't until his student, Pedro Rizzo, entered the Octagon a few years later that the fans of the sport saw just how dominant a striker could be. Backing up his punches and kicks with take-down defense, submission escapes, and a general knowledge of wrestling, Rizzo would begin the era of the striker by defeating Mark Coleman, a wrestler who had for so long been the alpha male of the sport.

The Rock

Sixty seconds into his bout with Tank Abbott on October 16, 1998, in UFC Ultimate Brazil, Pedro Rizzo could hear thousands of his compatriots cheering his name, but he could not see them. After being hit with an overhand right, he lost the top half of his vision. Rizzo, knowing Abbott would surely knock him out if he lifted his chin, focused on his opponent's lower extremities and began throwing kicks. Backpedaling, he followed one leg kick after another, slowly chopping the street brawler down. And when he had Abbott right where he wanted him, stationary and in pain, Rizzo found his opponent's face in the darkness and landed a right cross that sunk Abbott's ship. It was something straight out of the Karate Kid—Rizzo had defeated one of the world's best knockout artists half blind.

While growing up in Rio de Janeiro, Brazil, Pedro Rizzo idolized any man brave enough to step into a ring and engage in hand-to-hand combat. In hopes of one day following in their footsteps, he began training in judo in 1977 at the age of three. But on discovering that judo didn't possess the strikes necessary to knock out an opponent, he moved on to capoeira, a Brazilian martial art, at the age of eight. A natural at kicking and punching, he excelled in the discipline and soon found himself teaching others. Day and night he practiced various sweeps and flowery strikes, but in order to one day achieve his dream of fighting professionally, he felt he still had to learn more. That's when he approached his father about beginning kickboxing classes.

Pedro's father did not take the request well. As one of the most respected engineers in Brazil, he had always expected that Pedro would go to college and then pursue a professional career. He didn't want his son taking kicks and punches to the head and jeopardizing his future. So when Pedro continued to pester him, his father put his foot down and forbade his son from partaking in what he considered a barbaric and dangerous sport.

Pedro was not in the habit of disobeying his father—he loved the warm and comfortable lifestyle his family shared—but eventually the desire to learn the true fighting arts became too great, and he went searching for a school against his father's wishes. Just a few months after his father's lecture, Rizzo caught a bus to a rough neighborhood in Rio de Janeiro and visited a school run by a local fighting legend named Marco Ruas.

The training facility was like nothing Rizzo had ever seen. A ring sat in one corner, with the canvas stained with blood. The students weren't

After absorbing Tank Abbott's powerful right hand, Pedro Rizzo is partially blinded for the remainder of the bout.

wearing gis (uniforms), but rather street clothes, and instead of practicing forms and timed blocks, they tore into one another with punches and kicks. Overseeing them all was Ruas, a tall, muscular man who taught vale tudo—a system of fighting where anything is permitted. Most other children from middle-class homes would have turned and run, but not Rizzo. This was exactly what he had been looking for.

Finding a way to attend classes without being caught by his father proved difficult. Fortunately, Ruas bonded with the young dreamer instantly, and he not only offered to accept the boy's meager lunch money in exchange for dues, but he also agreed to pick him up after school and drive him to the gym. In exchange for his instructor's generosity, Rizzo put all his focus into training. He dedicated his first months to learning how to kickbox. Ruas, however, saw great potential in the boy, and he wanted him to learn all aspects of the fight game. "Marco knew how to fight on the ground," said Rizzo. "He'd been doing this kind of sport in Brazil a long time before the UFC.

Pedro Rizzo chops Tank Abbott down with leg kicks.

He'd trained to become an MMA fighter, and so I think he understood that you not only have to be a good striker, but you also have to understand how to fight on the ground."

Rizzo excelled in both areas, but with kickboxing being his forte, he entered the Rio de Janeiro Kickboxing Championships to test his skills after only two years of instruction. "Everyone has fear," said Rizzo. "I don't think anyone who steps into the ring is totally confident. Fighting is a hard game, because no one goes in there to lose. Every time you get into the ring, you can expect a hard time, a hard fight. I don't have a fear of getting cut, knocked out, or injured. I have a fear of losing. So every time I get into the ring, I try to win as fast as possible."

In his first fight Rizzo did just that. With his opponent being the former state champion of Rio de Janeiro, Rizzo decided that trading punches with the battle-tested veteran wasn't the wisest

plan of attack. Instead, he unleashed a series of devastating kicks to his opponent's legs. Although to the majority of those in attendance, it seemed as though Rizzo were losing the fight, but Ruas knew otherwise. He instructed his student to continue with the kicks, and halfway through the second round, Rizzo's opponent gripped at his leg and dropped to the canvas. When the referee asked if he was done, the former state champion said that he was.

It was the biggest test Rizzo ever took, and he passed victoriously. "I see a lot of talent in the gym, but in the ring they are nothing," said Rizzo. "There are some guys you can never teach how to handle the fight itself. Either you like getting in there or you don't. You can teach someone to become a great fighter, a complete fighter, but if he doesn't truly want to fight, he is not going to win in the ring."

Knowing that he had the mindset, heart, and

Pedro Rizzo lands a knockout punch on Josh Barnett. "I hit him very hard," says Rizzo. "I had to have surgery on my hand after that."

courage to make his dream come true was one of the greatest realizations in Rizzo's life. He left the ring with all the confidence in the world, but once he got backstage and looked in the mirror, worry set in. During the course of battle he had been punched in the face numerous times, and a small cut had opened under his eye. For two years he had been able to hide his secret life from his father, but now the truth would come out into the open.

After a pep talk from his instructor, Rizzo began to see the positive side. If he was man enough to face an opponent in hand-to-hand combat, then he was man enough to face his father. He went home that day with a trophy in hand and explained his intentions of becoming a fighter. When his father gave him the familiar speech about making something of his life and becoming a professional, Rizzo told him that's exactly what he planned to do. But instead of becoming an engineer like his brother or a journalist like his sister, he would make his father proud by becoming a professional fighter.

To prove his desire, Rizzo entered another kickboxing bout just a week later and defeated his opponent in a similar fashion. Feeling as though nothing could stand in his way, he then traveled south to the booming city of São Paulo to accept a challenge from an unknown fighter. The fight, however, didn't go as anticipated. Instead of standing there and accepting his leg kicks, his opponent unleashed a flurry of savage combinations. Rizzo was rocked from punches and kicks high and low, falling to the canvas twice in the first round. Rattled and shaken, he desperately searched for a way to turn the tide, but before an answer presented itself, he took a devastating fist to the jaw.

Rizzo woke up in the shower. Looking up into his trainer's face, he asked what had happened. On learning that he had been knocked out, Rizzo began to cry, thinking that all his years of training and preparation had been for nothing. He became certain his career was over. Ruas, having trained dozens for competition over the years, quickly corrected him. He told his student that instead of losing he had learned a valuable lesson—one that every fighter eventually comes to understand—no one can come out on top all the time.

Trying to put the defeat in the past, he immediately returned to training. Rizzo worked on improving his technique and power, and he made such progress that just a few months later Ruas took him to a tournament in which one of the top Muay Thai instructors from Holland was giving a demonstration. The two were introduced, and after Rizzo offered a sample of his skills, the foreign instructor invited the young scrapper to come train with him in Holland.

Rizzo found himself at a crossroad. All his life he had dreamed about becoming a professional fighter, and now here was his opportunity. Going to Holland meant he would train with all the world champions and step into the ring with legends he had only seen on television. But despite all the sacrifices he'd made and all the hours he'd devoted to training with Ruas, he never fully committed to his goal. After high school, he had enrolled in college with the intention of becoming a veterinarian. In the back of his mind, he always thought there would be a way to do both—follow his dream and make his father proud.

To decide which road to take, all Rizzo had to do was look at his trainer. Ruas represented everything he wanted to be—strong, confident, and a champion in all aspects of the word. Although his father was also such a man, after

Pedro Rizzo chops away at Randy Couture's leg.

Fighting for position in the clinch, Pedro Rizzo lands a knee to Randy Couture's ribs.

years sweating and bleeding with Marco, Rizzo knew that he had been born a warrior, and to follow any other path would just lead to disappointment. The only time he felt truly alive was in the ring. "I don't get into the ring for money," said Rizzo. "I don't get in there to get famous. I get in there because that is where I want to be. People ask why I train so hard for months and months. They ask why I give up everything for a fight that only lasts for fifteen minutes. But I know why I do it. I want to have the chance to be the best."

Dropping out of college and leaving his homeland for the first time, Rizzo's life changed forever.

Trapped under Randy Couture, a bloody Pedro Rizzo struggles to stay in the fight.

No longer able to return to the warmth of his family after a hard day of training and no longer able to hear Ruas's encouraging words after suffering an injury or setback, Rizzo reached inside himself and pulled up the man who would one day make him a champion. He trained seven hours a day in Holland, building his immunity to pain, honing his skills, and strengthening his mind. Not able to afford rent, he slept on a mat in the corner of the gym. To feed himself, he worked security at various nightclubs in the city. The only thing that mattered was climbing into the ring, and soon that opportunity presented itself. Eight months after his arrival, he had racked up thirteen professional fights and knocked out some of the biggest names in the sport of kickboxing.

But despite his tremendous success overseas, Rizzo missed the company and guidance of his mentor. In his absence, Ruas had moved to Los Angeles, California, and entered UFC 7, held on September 8, 1995, and swept the entire tournament. "After Marco, the UFC changed," said Rizzo. "The stand-up fighters began training to fight on the ground, and the ground fighters learned how to fight standing up. That's when the level of the sport got higher and higher." Ruas had always talked about mixed martial arts (MMA) being the sport of the future, and now his predictions were coming true. Rizzo wanted to be there to support his instructor, and so he decided to leave Holland and head to Los Angeles.

Shortly after the two reunited, Ruas sat his student down. He told Rizzo that he was proud of all his accomplishments in Holland, but from the beginning he'd always had a greater vision for him. Not any of those years schooling him in wrestling and submissions had been a waste of

After a very close bout, Pedro Rizzo is surprised to learn that the judges have given Randy Couture the decision. "I thought I never could lose to Randy because I really think I am a better fighter than him," says Rizzo. "But you never know, the ring is the ring. The level of this sport is very high, and if you make the smallest mistake, you are going to pay for it."

time. From the first time they'd hit the mats together, he had been training Rizzo for MMA competition, and now, with the UFC in the international spotlight, it was his time to show the world that he was not just a champion kickboxer, but also a champion fighter—one who could dominate any competitor who stepped up to face him.

To have an opportunity to follow Ruas's example meant everything to Rizzo, and he said he would make his instructor proud. The two began training the next day, and soon Ruas brought Rizzo to meet the UFC matchmakers. A few days after the meeting, Rizzo received a telephone call asking if he wanted to compete in UFC Brazil. Rizzo instantly accepted, but before he got off the telephone, the UFC wanted to make it very clear who he would be fighting—the infamous Tank Abbott. "I didn't care," said Rizzo. "I told them I just came from Europe and fought with the best kickboxers in the world. If Tank tries to come and exchange punches and kicks with me, it will be no problem."

Rizzo was in the UFC, but there was a catch. Because of the amount of worthy applicants desiring to enter the show, if Rizzo wanted to be invited back he would have to win. With this in mind, he went to work with Ruas, who was scheduled to fight overseas in a promotion only a few days before Rizzo's UFC debut. The two worked on striking, submissions, and wrestling. They worked on counterpunching and getting back to their feet after being taken down. After he had trained under a man who he thought was larger than life, Rizzo thought there was nothing that could stop him from defeating Abbott before thousands of his compatriots.

At the end of many months of training, the two wished each other the best and parted company. Knowing Ruas would not be in his corner during his fight was hard to accept, but Rizzo knew his trainer would be there in spirit. To make sure he was prepared for the worst, he continued training even after Ruas had left, but during one of his sessions he clacked heads with a sparring partner, opening a deep cut under his eye. He ran to the bathroom, and when he saw blood running down his face he began to cry. His training partner, realizing what he had done, began to pray with his eyes closed. To keep himself from panicking, Rizzo also joined in and prayed.

A visit to the emergency room, which resulted in four stitches, only reinforced Rizzo's deepest fear—there was no way the cut would heal for his fight, which was less than a week away. To make matters worse, that evening he learned by telephone that Ruas had lost his bout overseas. In a matter of hours, he had gone from the peak of confidence to the depths of despair. Doubt began to circle his mind.

That night, however, Rizzo realized just how far he had come in the past ten years. Martial arts had taught him how to be confident and how to be a man, and if it could carry him past his childish ways, then it could also carry him through this dilemma. He thought back to his early years when he had trained with Ruas, how his instructor constantly encouraged him, telling him that there was no one who could beat him on his feet and that there was no one who could beat him on the ground. Rizzo was going to prove that in less than a week. He would win this one for Ruas.

At the fighters' meeting, Rizzo hovered in the background, hoping no one would notice the cut on his face. Luckily, he ran into Phyllis Lee, Dan Severn's former manager, and she suggested that he superglue the cut closed. He took her advice, and when he went through the doctor's inspection, the gash went unnoticed. But that didn't mean that the cut wouldn't reopen during the fight. In order to avoid a referee stoppage due to bleeding, he would have to end this one quick.

Other than getting hit with the overhand right that blinded him for the majority of the bout, Rizzo felt proud of his victory. "It was a dream come true to fight in UFC Brazil," said Rizzo. "It was against Tank, one of the biggest guys in the UFC. Everyone knows Tank Abbott. He had so many losses, but he always gave an exciting show. He knocked out many, many people and gave a hard time to almost everyone."

Rizzo wanted to share his triumph with those who meant the world to him—his family. Although his father still wasn't overjoyed that he stepped into the ring for a living, he had come to accept his son's path. After the fight, his entire family, including all his training partners, gathered together to celebrate the biggest victory of his life. The only thing that kept the moment from being complete was the absence of Ruas, but the two would see each other again soon. Together, they would carve their names in the history of MMA and the UFC.

Over the next two and a half years, Rizzo let his punches and kicks fly against the toughest heavyweight competitors the UFC had to offer. "When you are standing up, no one can hold you back in a fight," said Rizzo. "When you go to the ground, even if your opponent isn't that good, he can hold you down, and then you can't do anything. A competitor has the power to stop the fight on the ground, because he can just keep you in his guard and defend himself. But standing

Pedro Rizzo lands a right hook to the temple of Andrei Arlovski.

Seeing an opening, Pedro Rizzo lands a kick to the neck of Andrei Arlovski.

up, no one can stop the fight. It's hard to just hold, hold, hold. Standing up, you can punch the guy, can kick him, and can use knees and elbows. That's why I like stand-up—there is more action."

Rizzo demonstrated just how devastating an effective striker could be on January 8, 1999, when he defeated world-class wrestler and UFC powerhouse Mark "The Hammer" Coleman in UFC 18: *Road to the Heavyweight Title*, at the Pontchartrain Center in New Orleans. "He had lost his last two fights, and I knew he was going to come into his third fight trying to kill anyone who stepped in front of him," said Rizzo. "It was a great challenge for me. I told myself that I was

a fighter, and I couldn't choose my opponents. If I wanted to be a world champion, I had to beat everybody." To keep the wrestler from kicking his legs and hauling him to the canvas, Rizzo practiced more than two hundred sprawls a day. To prepare for the worst-case scenario, he also had his sparring partners trap him on his back against the fence, the very position in which Coleman disposed of the majority of his victims.

Although Coleman managed to take him down several times on the night of the fight, Rizzo weathered the assault and escaped back to his feet, landing enough strikes to earn a decision by the judges. It was a great victory, but Rizzo

Pedro Rizzo lands a jab on the powerful Russian wrestler Vladimir Matyushenko.

and for the next two hours he rolled around with world-class wrestlers, avoiding takedowns, working for position, and struggling to get up off his back. At noon he took a break for food, but he returned to the gym at five o'clock for his cardio and weight-lifting workout. "I lift weights to get more explosive in my fights," said Rizzo. "I try to make my lifting movements the same that I would make in a fight, such as punching and kicking." Once he had his workout out of the way, he then returned to the mats to practice submission holds and striking on the ground.

On Tuesdays and Thursdays he focused primarily on striking. Instead of rolling on the mats in the morning, he threw on protective gear and sparred hard in both boxing and kickboxing. After lunch and a nap, he again returned to the gym at five o'clock for technical stand-up, wrestling, and then light sparring in the clinch. Rizzo trained for a twenty-five minute war because he knew Couture was doing the same.

For both competitors, it was the most important fight of their careers. And on the night of the fight, they fought accordingly. For twenty-five minutes the battle shifted back and forth, both fighters displaying the true meaning of heart. On the feet, Rizzo laid into Couture with punch/kick combinations and dropped the wrestler on several occasions. On the ground, Couture trapped Rizzo against the fence and unleashed a flurry of downward punches, elbows, and shoulder slams. In the history of the UFC, there had never been a more exciting match between a grappler and a striker, and although many thought the fight had been too close to call, the judges saw otherwise. With both warriors standing up battered and bloodied in the middle of the ring, Rizzo watched as Couture's hand was raised.

Rizzo traveled home to Brazil, and being with his friends and family allowed him to put the defeat into perspective. Out of forty-five professional fights, it had only been his third loss. He went back into training, and before he knew it, the UFC telephoned him and said that his fight with Couture had been so close, and such a draw with the fans, that they wanted to schedule a rematch at UFC 34, held on November 2, 2001. Rizzo told them that as long as Couture was willing to fight, then so was he.

Their second encounter, however, didn't possess the magic of their first. Couture, having studied Rizzo's fighting style in the past months, completely dominated the fight both on the ground and on his feet. In the second round he split open Rizzo's face, and in the third round he took the striker to the ground, trapped him against the fence, and ended the bout with a series of crushing blows. "I didn't show up in the ring that night," said Rizzo. "I didn't lose to Randy Couture, I lost to myself. But you never know, the ring is the ring. In this sport the level is so high, if you make even the smallest mistake, you're going to pay for that. And I did. I paid for it that night."

Rizzo put the loss behind him and continued on in the UFC, but with the caliber of fighters competing in the heavyweight division continuing to increase, Rizzo found himself facing giants who could strike, grapple, and move with the speed of a lightweight. Couture, after being completely dominated by Ricco Rodriguez, made the move down to the light heavyweights, but for Rizzo this wasn't an option. "I'm one of the lightest heavyweights," said Rizzo. "Everyone is 245, 250. I'm 230. But I can't drop down to 205—I've tried already, but I can't. My bones are heavy, so

Pedro Rizzo displays the Brazilian flag as he receives a decision over Ricco Rodriguez.

it is very hard to drop down." As a result, Rizzo found himself desperately trying to stay afloat in the heavyweight division. After defeating Andrei Arlovski on March 22, 2002, in UFC 36, he suffered two defeats in the Octagon, one to Gan McGee on September 27, 2002, in UFC 39, and the other to Vladimir Matyushenko on February 28, 2003, in UFC 41.

To avenge his losses, he reentered the Octagon and defeated Tra Telligman on June 6, 2003, in UFC 43, and then went on to receive a decision by the judges over Couture's former conqueror, Ricco Rodriguez on November 21, 2003, in UFC 45. "Right now in my career, I have the biggest pressures," said Rizzo. "I still think I'm one of the best, but I've had a bad time the last two years. I have a lot of pressure on my shoulders, but I can't think about how I need to win for the crowd or the fans. I think about how I need to win for myself. I want to be the best again. I have improved in all aspects of the game. You have to be great on the ground, you have to be a great wrestler, you have to be great at everything. Of course, it is hard to become 100 percent flawless in all these areas, but you have to try. You have to always try to be perfect."

But no matter what fate awaits Rizzo in the Octagon, to those who love him the most, he will always be that little boy who loves the martial arts.

The Iceman

In a three-year period, Chuck Liddell stepped into the Octagon on six separate occasions with the top light heavyweight fighters in the world, and on each occasion he came out in triumph. For some time he had been the number-one contender to take on Tito Ortiz for the title belt, but Ortiz was not looking forward to Liddell's lightning-fast punches, kicks, and knees. Instead of waiting around for Ortiz to step up to the plate, Liddell continued to battle inside the Octagon. He had first entered the UFC for the challenge, and despite all the fame he acquired in recent years, his primary reason for competing had never changed. Even though a loss would jeopardize his ranking, he took on Renato Sobral on November 22, 2002, in UFC 40.

Just as in his previous six bouts, Liddell proved why he deserved a shot at the title. Hunting Sobral around the ring, he landed a series of jabs, hooks, and overhand rights, softening up his opponent. Then, in a wild exchange of fists only three minutes into the bout, Liddell snuck in a high roundhouse kick that clashed into the forehead of Sobral, knocking him unconscious. With this victory under his belt, Liddell felt surely there was no way Ortiz could duck him any longer.

Although Chuck Liddell spent his early years enthralled by the television show *Kung Fu Theater*, he didn't start seriously training in the martial arts until he was attending college at Cal Poly, San Luis Obispo, California. Between his tedious studies and hours of grueling wrestling practice, Liddell somehow mustered the time and energy to learn kenpo karate. He discovered that he had a natural talent for throwing punches and kicks, and not long after he started, he began entering professional kickboxing matches. "That was the hardest thing, trying to get good grades and being able to train to fight at the same time," said Liddell. "People don't re-alize just how much time it takes to train, as well as the downtime you need after training that hard. You might be training four to six hours a day, but then you need a couple more hours just to sit there and relax. In college I majored in business accounting, and so it was a rough ride."

Despite the mental and physical strain, Liddell stuck with the sport, and he quickly racked up twenty-two professional bouts. Known as the "Iceman" for his lack of fear, he developed quite a reputation in the fight world, and then one day a promoter asked him if he would be interested in competing in (mixed marital arts) MMA. With both a wrestling and kickboxing background, it

Chuck Liddell lands a right cross to the face of Kevin Randleman.

seemed like a natural progression to Liddell, and so a short while later he entered an MMA tournament in Las Vegas, California. His opponent was touted as a submission expert, but that didn't stop Liddell from knocking him out with a hard roundhouse kick to the head. With this impressive victory under his belt, he caught the attention of UFC promoters, and they added him as an alternate to the card of UFC 17 on March 5, 1999.

Sporting his usual Mohawk and goatee, Liddell made a big impression on the spectators by winning a decision by the judges after beating on his opponent Noe Hernandez with a variety of strikes. Promoters realized that Liddell had both the talent and look to become a star in the sport, and they decided to place him on the main card of UFC 19, held on March 5, 1999. His opponent was Jeremy Horn, a fighter who had come out of nowhere and given Frank Shamrock, a master

submission master and brother to Ken Shamrock, heavy competition in UFC 17. After Horn's impressive debut with Shamrock, it was no secret that he possessed an arsenal of submissions holds; so on fight night, Liddell came right out of the gates firing with strikes. To the surprise of Liddell, Horn managed to stay with him on the feet. He chopped away at Liddell's legs with kicks, and then threw a foot up high, catching Liddell in the head.

This angered Liddell more than hurt him, and perhaps Horn understood this, because immediately after landing the high kick, he closed the gap and went for the takedown. Liddell's wrestling prowess kicked in, and while fending off Horn, he managed to land a handful of punches. Horn was persistent, however, and he eventually managed to haul the experienced striker to the ground.

Liddell didn't want to be lying on his back. He wanted to strike Horn and knock him out. Defending one submission attempt after another, he kept working back to his feet, but every time he threw a strike, Horn would take him down again. Eleven minutes into the match, Liddell finally ran out of escapes. Using wrestling technique, he managed to roll Horn and achieve the top position, but in the process, Horn had gripped onto his head. Liddell's arm was trapped against his own throat, shutting down the blood flow to his brain. He knew the match only had fifteen seconds left, and he was certain he could ride the chokehold out. But when the referee separated them after the bell rang, Liddell didn't rise. He had passed out.

This was Liddell's first loss in an MMA competition, and he wanted to make sure that it would be his last. To learn how to better defend against the takedown, he went back to the beginning. "I got a bunch of wrestlers to throw headgear on and try to take me down while I was throwing blows," said Liddell. "If I was going to be fighting three five-minute rounds, I'd try to do at least four rounds in training. I did a lot of stuff from the half guard, and I did a lot of different jiu-jitsu drills. I just used jiu-jitsu as a way to get back to my feet rather than looking for submissions."

After his loss, Liddell became a new man in the Octagon. He launched an impressive string of victories by splitting open the face of shoot-fighter Paul Jones on September 24, 1999, in UFC 22: *There Can Be Only One Champion*. He went on to earn a decision by the judges on December 16, 2000, in UFC 29: *Defense of the Belts*, by chopping Jeff Monson down with kicks to the leg. One of his most impressive victories came next, when he

Chuck Liddell throws a stiff jab at Amar Suloev.

Vitor Belfort catches Chuck Liddell's leg kick.

fought Kevin Randleman in UFC 31. He dropped the aggressive wrestler with a single right cross to the face. In UFC 33, he defeated the dangerous Brazilian fighter Murilo Bustamante, and then he was awarded a decision by the judges in UFC 35 over fellow kickboxer Amar Suloev. Liddell seemed unstoppable, and thousands of fans couldn't wait to see him square off with Tito Ortiz, the light heavyweight champion.

There was little question that Liddell deserved a shot at the title, but each time promoters tried to arrange the match, Ortiz was either injured or claimed he had other commitments. Many people began to suspect that Ortiz was dodging the fight, especially since rumors had begun to circulate that when he'd trained with Liddell he hadn't been able to take him down. There was

little question as to which fighter had the better hands.

To prove that the fans mattered more than the title, Liddell continued to step into the Octagon even though no belt was on the line. "I enjoy fighting, and that is why I do it," said Liddell. He showed this by earning a unanimous decision in Las Vegas on June 22, 2002, in UFC 37.5: *As Real As It Gets*, against Vitor Belfort. He knocked out Renato Sobral in UFC 40 with a kick to the head. Liddell would have probably gone on forever without getting a shot at the title, but promoters of the UFC didn't think he should have to do that. After Ortiz defended his title against Ken Shamrock in UFC 40, they tried again to arrange the match. As usual, however, Ortiz had prior commitments.

Chuck Liddell throws a spinning heel kick to the liver of Vitor Belfort.

Enough was enough. With Randy Couture moving down from the heavyweight division, promoters arranged a match between Couture and Liddell, and the winner would get the interim title belt. If Ortiz wanted to maintain his spot on top of the mountain, he would have to climb into the Octagon to get it.

It was the chance Liddell had been waiting for, but after so many knockouts and victories over the past three years, he finally had an off night. Couture took him down at will and beat on him with punches and ruthless elbows. And when Liddell managed to regain his footing, Couture was right in front of him, landing punch after punch. "When I look back at the tape, I realize that it wasn't me fighting in there," said Liddell.

"I don't know who that was, but it wasn't me. Not to take anything away from Couture, he fought a great fight. I just didn't show up that night."

It was a hard blow to take after waiting for so long, but even though Liddell didn't have a belt strapped around his waist, it didn't change how he felt about the sport. He first became involved in MMA because he had thrived on hand-to-hand combat and wanted to test his skills. With the competition in the UFC only growing tougher, his love for the sport only grows deeper. He has no plans of retiring from the Octagon at any time soon, ensuring that his fans will get to see one of the greatest knockout artists in the UFC work his magic for some time to come.

Chuck Liddell blasts Renato Sobral with a reaching right cross.

The Martial Arts Superhero

Eddie Ruiz, a protégé of the infamous Tank Abbott, had big plans for Yves Edwards in UFC 43, held on June 6, 2003. Having a strong background in both wrestling and brawling, Ruiz didn't want to end the fight with a submission, and he didn't want to earn a decision by the judges. "I want to take his soul," Ruiz said in his prefight interview. "I want to beat him until he is done."

This would not be an easy goal to accomplish. Edwards could wrestle, he could grapple, and he could land a submission out of nowhere. But even though he was a smooth operator on the ground, his most dangerous quality as a fighter was his strikes. Edwards was the future of mixed martial arts (MMA), and over the course of his three-round fight with Ruiz, he displayed all his skills. He landed a flying knee and a solid roundhouse kick to Ruiz's face. He dominated the clinch, shooting forward one painful knee after the next. On the ground, he reversed his opponent effortlessly, climbing into the mount almost at will. He moved from one submission to the next—triangle chokes to arm bars to guillotine chokes. It was a tremendous showcase of skill, reminding all those who were watching not only how far the sport of MMA had come since the early days but also why strikers had made such a dramatic comeback in recent years.

Yves Edwards was raised by his mother and grandmother in the Bahamas, but it was his uncle who unknowingly helped Edwards decide that he wanted to become a martial arts superhero when his uncle brought home a videotape of the original *Superman* with Christopher Reeve and a copy of Bruce Lee's *Enter the Dragon*. Edwards watched both movies back to back, utterly enthralled by what he was seeing. He practiced lying on his back and springing to his feet like Bruce Lee, and he spent hours sifting through any comic book he could find. Although he idolized all superheroes, Batman soon became his favorite. "He has no powers at all," said Edwards, "and yet he will go toe-to-toe with anyone and ultimately come out on top."

After his mother had remarried and moved the family to Houston, Texas, Edwards began studying Chinese kung fu in an attempt to achieve his dream. He threw whirling kicks and open-hand strikes, thinking it was the deadliest fighting style in the world. Then he saw the first UFC on videotape. "At first I didn't understand why no one threw any spinning kicks," said Ed-

Yves Edwards struggles to keep Matt Serra from taking him to the ground.

Matt Serra strikes Yves Edwards in the back with an elbow.

Matt Serra attempts to apply a rear naked choke on Yves Edwards.

Matt Serra looking to apply a leg lock on Yves Edwards.

wards, "because that is what I was doing at the time."

Instead of making excuses as to why kung fu had failed when pitted against Gracie Jiu-Jitsu, Edwards decided to discover what grappling was all about. When he went back to the Bahamas to visit friends and family at seventeen years of age, he discovered that there was a ninjitsu school close by. The discipline didn't possess the intricate submissions of jiu-jitsu, but it focused more on ground fighting than Chinese kung fu.

On his first visit to the gym, he climbed onto the mat with a much smaller opponent who was only fourteen years old, and within minutes Edwards found himself gasping for air. All his flashy kicks and punches were worthless once he had been taken to the ground. With his opponent's arm wrapped around his neck, there was nothing he could do to defend himself.

Being so vulnerable didn't sit well with his superhero aspirations, so Edwards began studying mixed martial arts (MMA) shortly thereafter. Instead of practicing how to peck out an attacker's eyes with his fingertips, he learned how to capture an arm between his legs and extend it to the point of breaking. Instead of training to strike an aggressor with the ridge of his hand, he learned how to throw combinations straight down the pipe (i.e., straight, powerful punches). After a year of training, feeling he was getting closer to becoming a martial arts superhero, Edwards decided to enter a local vale tudo tournament that allowed only open-hand strikes to the face.

The night before the event, however, Edwards couldn't sleep or eat. He had spent his whole life trying to avoid physical confrontation, and now he was voluntarily stepping into one. For many hours he questioned if this was the path that he wanted to take, and by morning he realized that it was. Although the fear of losing was great, the fear of failing himself by not stepping up to the plate was even greater. "I entered the tournament at a 147 pounds, and got my butt kicked for twenty minutes," remembered Edwards. "It was a horrible feeling. I was trapped in an arm lock for about fifteen minutes, but even though I couldn't get out, I wasn't going to quit. I remember hearing someone say that there were two minutes left, and I thought to myself, 'OK, you've got two minutes to figure out a way to beat this guy.'" Unfortunately, Edwards didn't yet have the skills or the strength.

After suffering a defeat at his first competition, Edwards languished in depression for several days. When he finally went back to the gym and all his training partners offered their support, he realized that while he had lost, he'd had fun out there on the mat, struggling to put his opponent away. It motivated him to train harder and to plug the holes in his technique. "I got mounted a couple of times in the fight, and I didn't know how to get off my back," said Edwards. "And so I needed to learn some mount escapes. I also needed to learn how to keep myself from getting submitted. The only reason the guy didn't finish me with the arm lock was because he was also an amateur. He was just as new as I was, but he was a whole lot stronger. So in addition to everything else, I also had to work on my strength, lift some weights, and learn how to eat right. Even back then, I had to start learning how to eat right to help my body stay strong."

Watching his skill level and power improve daily made Edwards anxious to get back into the ring to avenge his loss. And when he entered another local tournament a few years later, he did just that, submitting his opponent with a rear

Carrying Matt Serra on his back, Yves Edwards guards against the choke and remains calm. "I lost my fight with Serra because of tentativeness," says Edwards, "and I have never been tentative since."

naked choke. The victory felt like a drug, and from that moment on he was devoted to MMA competition. "I knew I wanted to be a fighter at that point," said Edwards. "I took a year of my life and I didn't go out, I didn't hang out with my friends. I had two roommates who also trained, and they were still into partying. They wanted to hang out and have fun—I just wanted to get better, and that is what I did. All I did was go to

work and then go to the gym. That was my life for a whole year. I didn't want anything different."

His determination paid off. While the majority of his friends spent their weekends attending house parties, Edwards traveled to MMA competitions around the country and racked up over a dozen victories, the majority by way of knockout or submission.

During his travels, Edwards was fortunate

With Caol Uno clinging to his back, Yves Edwards takes a moment to rest. "Uno was one of those guys who I thought was a superstar, and I didn't think I was anywhere near his level," says Edwards. "I still think he is a great fighter, but now I know that I'm on his level."

enough to meet many of the legends in the sport, including Bas Rutten, Marco Ruas, and Tito Ortiz. "These guys were either on the cusp of becoming superstars or they were already superstars," said Edwards. "I met these guys, and they would talk to me like I was on their level. They were always throwing my name out to other promoters, and I think Tito was the first guy to tell Joe Silva, the UFC matchmaker, about me. That made things a lot easier. Some guys don't get as lucky. There are some really big guys who have amazing fighting records, and yet nobody knows who they are."

Although it was Ortiz's referral that got the

UFC to take a closer look, it was Edwards' skill that got him into the most respected MMA competition on earth. His submission and wrestling skills were comparable to that of any lightweight fighter in the UFC, but his hand speed and kicking power were downright unnatural. "I prefer the stand-up game just because there are very few guys out there who I feel can stand up with me," said Edwards. "When standing you can't do things on the fly. You have to be good at making decisions. On the ground, you can take more time to set things up—you can plot and be a lot more methodical. I like both aspects of the game, but I prefer stand-up simply because that is where I am the strongest."

With such accurate and powerful strikes, Edwards had little problem dominating the top opponents on a local level. But landing his infamous shots on UFC competitors would be a much more formidable task. When he received a telephone call from the UFC to say that they were going to give him a chance on September 28, 2001, in UFC 33 against Matt Serra, one of the top submission artists in the world, Edwards immediately stepped up his training. "Pretty much anyone who starts fighting in MMA competition wants to fight in the UFC," said Edwards. "That was my goal. I wanted it so bad, even before I was ready. And when I finally got the call, I was so happy. It didn't matter who I was fighting. If there were no weight classes and they wanted me to fight Tito, I would have done it in a heartbeat. I knew that Zuffa only wanted the best fighters, and so I was honored that they thought of me. There are billions of people in this world, and less than sixty of them have ever competed in the UFC. That meant a lot. It was the chance of a lifetime, so I did everything I could to prepare."

After waking up at six-thirty every morning to a three-mile run and a light breakfast, Edwards headed off to the MMA training facility he had opened in Woodland, Texas, to work on boxing with Kenny Weldon, one of Evander Hollyfield's primary trainers. "Kenny has a philosophy that boxing is hitting your opponent with the maximum amount of leverage from the farthest distance possible while exposing the least of yourself," said Edwards. "His style relies heavily on never being out of position. Your legs always have to be in the right place. It doesn't have much to do with hands at all, because your punches are just an extension of your legs. We do a lot of shadow boxing and various drills to improve the strength in my legs. He is real specific, and corrects me down to an inch of detail. Then he will do the same with my kicks. Although he is primarily a boxing coach, he gives me examples of how fighting on the ground is a lot like fighting on your feet. When you are boxing, your elbows are always in because it is the most powerful position. It's the same when you are grappling—you keep your elbows tucked in so you don't get submitted. So we work a lot on basic technique, and when he feels I'm ready to learn something new, he teaches me things like how to turn and pivot."

Edwards threw on the boxing gloves and stepped into the ring for hard sparring after he had focused on details for the first hour of training. Some days he stuck to straight boxing, and other days he threw kicks, knees, and elbows into the mix. He maintained a fast pace for eight to twelve rounds, facing a fresh opponent at the beginning of each three-minute period.

Exhausted from thirty minutes of straight battle, Edwards stepped up practice another notch as he began his ground work. For starters, he grabbed an experienced boxer who understood

Yves Edwards knocks Joao Pierini to the mat with a roundhouse kick to the head. "It surprised me that he didn't go to sleep," says Edwards. "A lot of people go to sleep when they get hit like that."

Yves Edwards crouches down to finish Joao Pierini off with strikes.

how to sprawl, and then he slapped the sixteen-ounce gloves on him. The boxer's job was to try to take Edwards' head off, and Edwards' job was to bring him down somehow to the canvas. After twenty minutes of this, the rolls were reversed. Edwards threw on the gloves and had to avoid being brought to the mat. If he was taken down, he wasn't allowed back to his feet. His opponent rode his weight on top of him, in either the mount or the guard position, and then landed as many shots as possible. To survive, Edwards had to either escape or submit his opponent. "You are constantly going," said Edwards. "We have four guys in the ring at a time. As soon as you get up from one guy, somebody else is instantly on you. As soon as you take the boxer down, then he gets on top of you and mounts you. As soon as you get out of that, someone is shooting a double trying to take you down. If they get you down, they are trying to submit you."

The entire training session lasted a brutal three hours, and after it was over, Edwards quickly headed home for lunch and a nap. But at seven-thirty in the evening, after taking a bike ride and teaching his evening classes, the mental and physical abuse started all over again. "We do a lot more sparring," said Edwards. "Sometimes we will put on the MMA gloves and spar with MMA rules. But we don't go as hard as we did in the morning. We are working more for submissions than punches. Sometimes we won't even put the gloves on; we'll just wrestle for an hour straight without any breaks."

At ten o'clock at night, the training was finally over, and Edwards returned home to get much needed sleep. But as the night of the fight grew closer, even the dark hours were filled with images of the upcoming battle. "Every night for a

couple of weeks out, I visualize the fight in my mind," said Edwards. "I can see myself in the Octagon, and I can almost feel like I'm really there in that environment and atmosphere. I'll start to get butterflies in my stomach, but once I hear the ref say, 'Are you ready? Are you ready? Let's get it on!' all the nerves go away. I get that feeling for a few seconds and it calms me down. It makes me feel ready to fight."

By the time Edwards traveled to Las Vegas, Nevada, for the fight, he had already won the battle a hundred times. To warm up, he did the same thing that he always did in the gym to get started. "After I stretch, I like to wrestle around a little bit and work the pads. Sometimes, depending on whom I am fighting, I'll do fifteen minutes of warm up," said Edwards. "I'll get one of my training partners and we'll have a slow fight. Of course we're not going 100 percent, but we are going at least 20 percent. They will help me work and build up a sweat so I can get to the cusp of that second wind, but not quite break into it."

Once his name was called, Edwards headed down the aisle toward the Octagon, followed by his three chosen cornermen. While many MMA fighters chose to have their closest partners on the sidelines, Edwards always chooses those who will help him most throughout the fight. First, he likes to have someone who is knowledgeable in the sport and can tell him everything he needs to know, such as how to get off his back if an opponent is keeping him down. Then he will have his boxing coach who instructs him while he is in the standing position. "He focuses on me being in the right position and doing the right things," said Edwards. "He also tries to pick apart my opponent. If he says something, I do it. I don't try to set it up. If he says, 'throw a kick,'

Yves Edwards hits
Rich Clementi with a
powerful right cross.

Yves Edwards
reminds Rich
Clementi why he
is considered one
of the best strikers
in the lightweight
division.

Mounted on top of Rich Clementi, Yves Edwards picks his shots.

I do it right then without hesitation." Third, Edwards always brings along a motivator who watches the time and says things like, "You have thirty seconds left; you have to get off your back!"

When Edwards stepped into the Octagon, he felt confident, yet at the same time he also felt that he needed to be cautious. He had seen videotapes of Matt Serra's fights, and he understood just how dangerous Serra could be on the ground. Edwards felt that if the fight was to go to the ground, there was no chance for him to win. So when the fight began, he found himself playing it overly safe, trying to avoid any sign of the takedown. This, however, not only took away from his striking capability, it also took away points on the judges' scorecards. At one point near the end of the first round, Edwards decided he had to do something, and for the first time in

the fight he was truly unleashed. "I rocked him with an uppercut and put him on his back," said Edwards. "I mounted him briefly, but then I backed out of it. He was dazed, his bell was rung, and I should have kept tagging him, but I didn't, simply because I wanted to stay away from the ground. All my training focused on staying off the ground, and during the fight that was all I could think about."

After taking a few of Edwards' strikes, Serra began pulling his opponent down into his guard every chance he got, going for one submission after another. Edwards defended himself flawlessly, and every time he saw an opening, he scrambled back to his feet. The entire match was a back-and-forth battle, but when the bout was put into the hands of the judges, Serra was awarded the unanimous decision. It didn't take long for Edwards to realize the mistakes he had

Yves Edwards lands a flying knee to the face of Eddie Ruiz.

Tightening his hooks around the waist of Eddie Ruiz, Yves Edwards works for a rear naked choke.

made. "I'm glad that it turned out the way it did, because I take a few more risks now," said Edwards. "They are still calculated risks, but I'm no longer afraid of doing things I shouldn't be afraid to do. I have never lost the same way twice. I lost the fight with Matt Serra because of my tentativeness, and I have never been tentative since. If you get an 'L' on your record and don't learn anything from it, then that 'L' stands for a loss. But if you get an 'L' on your record and it changes you as a fighter, then it stands for a learning experience."

When Edwards returned to the Octagon in UFC 37: *High Impact*, held on May 10, 2002, at Bossier City, Louisiana, he planned to correct those mistakes in the ring with Caol Uno, even though his opponent was just as dangerous on the ground as Serra had been. He planned to take it to his opponent with strikes, despite the risk of

being taken down, but Uno had apparently anticipated this. Instead of squaring up with Edwards, Uno chose to take a sideways stance that gave Edwards only a narrow target to aim for. Edwards was thrown off by his unconventional stance, and inevitably the fight went to the ground.

Instead of backing out and up to his feet as he had done in his previous bout, Edwards went for submissions. In the process of doing this, however, Uno managed to reverse him several times and take control. "I was trying not to be afraid of anything, not be afraid of going to the ground," said Edwards. "But at the same time, Uno is kind of tricky. He is real smart and plays the game well. Sometimes he would get me in moves that I wasn't familiar with, and I was hesitant because I didn't know what he could do with those moves."

Yves Edwards parries a right cross from Nick Agallar.

Yves Edwards lands a kick to the leg of Nick Agallar.

When the fight was on the feet, Edwards clearly dominated, even though he didn't land any knockout punches. On the ground, he went for submissions and escaped those applied by Uno. Neither of them could pull out a finish, and once again Edwards found his fate being handed to the judges. Edwards felt that he had won, and he was shocked to hear that Uno had received a unanimous decision. "I think that fight could have gone either way, and I think Uno would agree with that," said Edwards. "When the first judge ruled the fight for him, Uno put his hand up because he was happy. Then the second judge ruled the fight in his favor, and the look on his face was that of utter surprise. He was completely surprised, and so was I."

Edwards now had two losses in the UFC. He knew if he was going to remain in the greatest MMA show on earth, then he had to pull out a win at the next show. He took the first opportunity he got to step back into the Octagon, which happened to be in UFC 37.5, held on June 22, 2002. His opponent was Joao "The Tasmanian Devil" Pierini, a second-degree black belt in jiu-jitsu. Edwards planned on going into the bout like a savage, but backstage he ran into some

A disoriented Nick Agallar covers up as Yves Edwards comes in for the kill.

Mounted on Nick Agallar, Yves Edwards searches for the most vulnerable spot.

unexpected difficulties. "Five minutes before the fight started, I was throwing up," said Edwards. "It was a little bit of nerves, and I ate some bad cheese the day before the weigh-in. I had some Italian food that didn't agree with me. I've seen a lot of things like that backstage, things the fans never get to see while watching on television. That is why I have respect for all the fighters. You never know what any of the fighters are going through, but they always come out no matter what. Even if they don't perform to the best of their abilities or as well as you have ever seen them perform, they are still giving it their all every time."

Likewise, Edwards was no different. When his name was called, he walked down the aisle of reaching fans and climbed into the Octagon. Pierini was primarily a grappler, and Edwards thought he would have to work to keep the fight standing, but in the opening seconds, the Brazilian fighter used his reach advantage to land two overhand rights that opened a small cut under Edwards' right eye. Instead of blindly retaliating, Edwards plotted his attack. "If you know someone is looking to take you down, it is a really bad idea to lead with a head kick because it leaves you standing on one foot," said Edwards. "The first attack is the easiest one to counter. If you put things into a combination, then it's a lot harder to take you down. It's just like driving on the freeway—anyone can drive on the freeway at three o'clock in the morning when no one is out, but you try to get to the same destination in the same amount of time during rush hour, it is going to be a lot harder."

Edwards began his assault by throwing two kicks to the leg. Then, with Pierini thinking about guarding the lower half of his body, Edwards went upstairs with a kick that nearly knocked the head off the jiu-jitsu stylist. "When I knock someone out, I usually know it's going to happen," said Edwards. "I can feel it, I can feel their game is not ready for mine. Seconds before, I know that the fight is going to be over pretty soon. With Pierini, I saw that he kept dropping his left hand whenever he threw a punch. I'm always looking for things like that; I'm watching how people bring their hands back after they throw punches. They might throw good punches, but sometimes they leave their hands low, or their chin is up in the air. I saw that Pierini was doing that, dropping his hands, and so I figured I was going to come in and fake a punch, he would drop his hand to pat it down, and I would throw a kick to the head. I'm not a big guy, but I'm sure there are guys who are a lot bigger than me who don't kick nearly as hard just because their technique is not right. You have to use the hips and turn the body over, same thing as boxing. Throwing punches and throwing kicks is the same, your attacks are just an extension of your hips. So I hit him pretty hard, and it surprised me that he didn't go to sleep. A lot of people go to sleep when they get hit like that. So I followed it up with some punches when I saw that he was still awake on the ground."

Knowing he didn't want to be drawn into a ground battle as he had with both Serra and Uno, Edwards backed away and stood up. Pierini managed to labor back to his feet, but after a quick visit with the ringside doctor, the fight was brought to a halt. In a minute and twenty seconds, Edwards had just won his first bout in the UFC, and in classic striker style. "It felt really good to get a win," said Edwards. "It made me feel good that Zuffa wanted me to come back again. At the same time, it showed some of my skills, things that I can do in a fight. It didn't show a lot, because the fight didn't last that long. What it did was it left the door open for me to come back and showcase some of my skills at a later date."

Edwards did just that. In UFC 41, held on February 28, 2003, he beat his opponent Rich Clementi from one side of the ring to the other and then showed his submissions skills when he sunk in a rear naked choke that forced his opponent to tap in submission. After that, it was the destruction of Eddie Ruiz in UFC 43, and then a TKO over Nick Agallar in UFC 45.

With four decisive victories under his belt, Edwards appears to have achieved his childhood dream of becoming a martial arts superhero, but he has tried to keep it in perspective. He knows that in this game, even the best fighters can be blindsided out of nowhere. "Just think about how much the game has evolved," said Edwards. "Just think about the kids who are five years old now watching the sport. In twelve or thirteen years from now, the sport is going to be completely different. There are going to be a whole bunch of martial arts superheroes running around."

The Maine-iac

When Tim Sylvia entered UFC 41, held on February 28, 2003, to take on heavy-weight champion Ricco Rodriguez for the title belt, few people took him seriously. They thought he would be no match for Rodriguez, the submission master who had put Randy Couture on his back, hit him with every strike known to man, and then walked away with his title belt. The general consensus was that Sylvia wouldn't last the first round. The odds makers in Las Vegas, Nevada, casinos agreed, and they had made Sylvia a five-to-one underdog. But what everyone somehow forgot to take into consideration was that Sylvia had been training seven days a week at Miletich Fighting Systems, a training camp that had produced UFC warriors such as Jens Pulver, Jeremy Horn, Matt Hughes, and Robbie Lawler. Bleeding and sweating with a group of warriors who had virtually owned the Octagon for the past three years, Sylvia couldn't have avoided learning some skills. On fight night, Sylvia planned to give all those watching one of the biggest upsets in UFC history.

While growing up in Eastbrook, Maine, Tim Sylvia was jumped, beaten up, and picked on. He had studied karate since he was barely old enough to stand, but he'd never actually had enough self-esteem to use the techniques he learned to protect himself. Then, shortly after a growth spurt shot him up to an amazing six feet eight inches during his senior year of high school, he saw the first UFC on videotape, and he was astounded by the bravery of the fighters. "I thought I would try that Royce Gracie stuff," said Sylvia. "I started doing it just for fun, and I picked it up because I had a little bit of a wrestling background. I did some tournaments, and I took first place in them. Somehow I got onto a mailing list at one of those events, and

they invited me to enter an amateur NHB fight in Rhode Island."

Sylvia debated whether he should compete. Entering a grappling tournament was one thing, but entering a no holds barred (NHB) fight was something else entirely. His size had given him some courage that he didn't have while growing up, but the thought of competing in a real fight before a crowd sent shivers down his spine. In the end, however, he concluded that entering the event would be the best thing to help him overcome his fear of confrontation. "I was scared as hell," remembered Sylvia. "I just got in there, and I saw this kid coming after me. I threw a leg kick as he threw a right hand, and I dropped him. I pounced on top of him, and hit him as many times as I could. Next thing I know, they're pulling me off him. I had to stop and think, 'Am I going to get in trouble for this?' When I realized I wouldn't, I wanted to do it again."

After his victory, Sylvia found the confidence he never thought he would have. He became determined to become a professional fighter, but taking the next step proved difficult. Maine didn't have a host of martial arts trainers, and it had even fewer trainers knowledgeable about mixed martial arts (MMA) competition. Discouraged but not defeated, Sylvia began attending every jiu-jitsu seminar that came through town. He watched countless UFC videotapes, studying the moves of his favorite champions such as Pat Miletich. He had learned some things, but he was still far from having the skills that could classify him as a professional. Getting frustrated with his goal, he decided to fly to Cedar Rapids, Iowa, and attend UFC 26, hoping to find some inspiration.

After purchasing general admission tickets to the event, Sylvia got in line four hours before the show started to make sure he would get good seats. While he was waiting, a few of the event's promoters approached him. They had mistaken him for Gan McGee, a six foot ten inch tall competitor who was scheduled to compete in the heavyweight division at a future event. Sylvia was about to correct them, but when they cleared a path and opened the door to the auditorium, he gladly played along.

"When I walked in, I saw Pat Miletich, Matt Hughes, and Jens Pulver all hanging out," said Sylvia. "I also saw Tito, but when I went up to him, he snubbed me. Then I went over to Pat, and he was like, 'Wow, you're a big son of a bitch.' We started shooting the shit, and I told him I was looking for a place to train. That's when he invited me to come down to Iowa and work out with him for a week."

Tim Sylvia lands a knee to the stomach of Wesley Correira.

Tim Sylvia rocks Wesley Correira's head with a right cross.

As the event got underway, Sylvia was so excited he could hardly sit still. He imagined what it would be like training with Miletich, Jeremy Horn, Pulver, Hughes, and all the other MMA champions he had watched on television for so many years. If there was anywhere he could learn the tools to become a professional MMA fight, it was at Miletich Fighting Systems, the most feared and respected MMA training facility in the world.

Sylvia knew enough about Miletich's camp to realize that the invitation was unconditional. If he couldn't handle the training, then he was welcome to leave the day he arrived. But if he was mentally and physically strong enough to endure the punishment that they dished out over the course of a week, then he was free to stay around as long as he wished. That was his goal, to become ultimately a part of their team. "I left everyone I knew, all my friends and family," said Sylvia. "I drove over twenty-four hours to Iowa, not knowing if I could make it or not. Not knowing if I had what it took to become a fighter. I just wanted to try, and I gave it everything. Everything."

But everything Sylvia had, including his height, weight, and strength, didn't come close to matching the ferocity of the more seasoned fighters in the gym. During his first several practices he was beaten repeatedly in the ring and on the mat. He was submitted with arm bars and chokeholds. He fell over in the weight room, and fell behind on the team's three-mile runs. His car was parked outside, his bags were packed, and yet he wouldn't give up. "Tim Sylvia was the exact opposite of Matt Hughes," said Monte Cox, manager for the Miletich Team. "When we saw Matt, we knew where he was headed. There was no doubt in our minds. The guy was a superior athlete, and we knew that with the right training he could be a champion. When Tim came to us, I

Tim Sylvia throws a cross as Ricco Rodriguez comes in with a knee. "I hit him a few times, and he shied away because he didn't like it," says Sylvia. "I thought, 'Sooner or later I'm going to get a hold of this guy.'"

misread him completely, and I'm a good judge of talent. I didn't think that he had a chance to be anything. He was so uncoordinated, so over-weight, throwing up in practice everyday. He just didn't have anything that would tell you he was going to be someone."

But Sylvia had heart, and it carried him through the first month of practice. Vomiting every day, however, was not his idea of a good time, and he realized very quickly that he needed to drop weight. "Back when I was in Maine, I didn't have time to eat healthy," said Sylvia. "I

had my own business. I was subcontracting out paint jobs, and I was putting in eight or nine hours a day. I was on the road so many hours, I didn't have time to pack a bunch of small meals, and eat every three hours like I was supposed to. But when I started training with Miletich, I knew that had to change. I went through a lot of grilled chicken, rice, and vegetables. That was pretty much all I ate three or four times a day."

His weight began to drop and his condition-ing and endurance slowly increased. He wanted to be able to give something back to his team-

As Ricco Rodriguez throws a kick to the leg, Tim Sylvia counters with a powerful punch.

mates who had carried him through practice. So in addition to going to the fighters' classes twice a day, Sylvia also began attending the classes open to the general public. "We have classes that are just takedown classes, so you have all these wrestlers coming in from colleges around the area," said Sylvia. "They are star wrestlers, and I would learn from them. Other nights, we have just grappling classes, and I would work out with the guys who are really good at jiu-jitsu. They might not want to fight or get into the ring, but they are really good at jiu-jitsu. Then we have sparring at night, and we have pro boxers come in who don't really want to get kicked. And so, I just boxed with those guys."

Working on his striking, wrestling, and sub-mission skills, Sylvia began to improve his over-all game, but in his mind nothing came fast enough. To better his footwork and explosiveness while sparring, he hired a strength-training coach who put him through plyometric workouts three times a week. For forty-five minutes straight, he would step from side to side, up onto a box and then down. Before he knew it, he was no longer lumbering around flatfooted in the ring. He was light on his feet, and when an opponent came at him, instead of going straight back, he would turn the corner on a dime.

Sylvia did everything he could think of on his own to help aid his advancement, but his true

As Ricco Rodriguez falls disoriented to the canvas, Tim Sylvia chases him down.

leaps and bounds were made during the fighters' training. "Everyone had a hand in his improvement," said Cox. "Pat is our stand-up coach, and so he worked on his boxing. Jeremy Horn worked a lot with him on his back, teaching him positioning and getting up. And then just the whole team, Matt Hughes and everyone, worked on his takedown defense. There was no one person who helped him get better. Pat will tell you it wasn't just him. It wasn't just Matt, and it wasn't just Jeremy. It was having them all together. Winning breeds winning, and success breeds success. When you are in a room with all these UFC champions, and all these tough guys, Tim just got it into his head that he was going to be like them. He thought, 'If I can start competing and doing well against these guys, then I can do well against anybody.' It's just a winning combination."

For two solid years, Sylvia breathed fighting. He didn't go out, and he didn't relax. Fighting was all he did or thought about. "When I was hurt, banged up, and injured, desire was the only thing that got me through," said Sylvia. "It's all about heart, having what it takes. Our gym isn't like most gyms. No matter how good I become, there will always be better strikers in my gym, there will always be guys who are better wrest-lers, and there will always be guys who are better grapplers. That is what is so great about our gym; on any given day you can get your ass kicked. But it is also hard. I often wondered if I could do it, if I had what it took. I broke down and cried many times."

But after thousands of hours in the gym and many life-altering sacrifices, all his training and hard work began to pay off. "When Tim first came to us, I didn't think he had what it took," said Cox. "But what I missed, which is often overlooked, is that Tim just had it in his head that he was going to be a champion. He kept

telling people the UFC heavyweight champion was just holding his belt for him, and we were like, 'This guy is clueless. He just doesn't have it.' He just kept working and working, and all these guys made fun of him. Everyone teased him. He didn't mind, he kept coming in and coming in. He never missed a practice, and he worked as hard as any heavyweight out there. Then, all of a sudden, he started beating people. He wasn't beating them real impressively, but he was beating them easier and easier."

Sylvia was excited about the small victories he garnered during practice, and he wanted to see how his skills would fare in a true MMA compe-

Tim Sylvia circles Ricco Rodriguez, looking to finish him off.

Tim Sylvia knocks Ricco Rodriguez out with a powerful punch.

tition. Although he still had a long way to go before he could even think about entering the UFC, Miletich agreed that he was ready for one of the smaller events, and he placed him in a promotion called the International Fighting Championships. "He barely won," said Cox. "He didn't fight very well. After that, I kind of took him over and started to put him in some of my shows. But to be honest, I thought, 'What am I going to do with this guy?' He was tough, but he just wasn't that coordinated, and on the ground he was going to be in trouble. His takedown de-

fense wasn't very good. Honestly, he fooled me. I've managed five UFC champions, I'm a pretty good judge, and he completely fooled me."

Despite what people said or thought, Sylvia kept fighting in local tournaments. Once he had competed in half-a-dozen bouts, five of which he won by way of knockout, everything started to come together. Both Cox and Miletich agreed that he was ready to step up to the next level, and they entered him in the Hawaiian Superbrawl, a fiercely competitive MMA elimination tournament. In order to take home the championship belt, he would have to win four separate bouts over the course of two days. "I went into that tournament very, very prepared," said Sylvia. "I did a lot of running for the event, ran my ass off. I just knew that my cardio was better than anyone else's was out there that day. Pat also helped me. He pulled me aside and said, 'Hey kid, you have come a long way, especially in striking. I don't want you taking these guys to the ground and pounding on them. Get after them on your feet. Work the sprawl, and let your hands go.' That is what I did. I knocked out every single guy I faced. It was great, absolutely great."

The entire Miletich camp couldn't have been more proud. They had watched Sylvia work so hard, make so many sacrifices, and now they couldn't be happier to see him reap the rewards. "You have to be mentally strong, and you have to know what you want," said teammate Hughes. "And then you have to go out there and work to get it. That's what it comes down to if you want to be a champion. A lot of people desire to be a world champion, but they wouldn't do what they need to do to become one." Sylvia had all those qualities right from the beginning, and he had proved it in the ring.

Cox realized he grossly underrated his fighter after he had watched Sylvia become a virtual knockout machine in the Superbrawl tournament. Just a few months later, he had a meeting with Joe Silva, the UFC matchmaker, and they added Sylvia to the card of UFC 39, held on September 27, 2002. Just as in his latest bouts, Sylvia earned a dramatic TKO over his opponent Wesley Correira. His victory impressed the UFC promoters so much, in fact, that they decided to give him a shot at Ricco Rodriguez, the current heavyweight champion of the world, in UFC 41, held on February 28, 2003.

It took awhile for reality to sink in, but once it did, Sylvia devoted himself to training like never before. "When I got ready to fight Ricco, it was five or six hours a day of hard training," said Sylvia. "My guys knew that Ricco didn't like to get hit. He was great on the ground, a superior grappler, and so that was the last place that I wanted to be with him. So my game plan was to keep the fight on the feet and not to do any kicking because it gave him an opportunity to take me down. If he was going to throw kicks, I was going to retaliate with the big right hand, which is the counter. I trained super hard, because no one outside of my training camp thought I could win that fight. They said that Ricco Rodriguez could take me in his sleep and that I didn't have enough fights in the UFC to be up for the title. Hearing that fueled my rage."

While the negative press inspired Sylvia, he realized that people believed those things for a reason, and the reason was that Rodriguez had a superior ground game. To prepare for Rodriguez's takedowns, Sylvia would put the gloves on his teammates and then try to stop them from taking him down. He would also put himself in many shady positions on the ground and then try to escape back to his feet while getting punched in the face. Sometimes he would be on his back for an hour straight, with two or three guys working in rotation throughout the practice.

Sylvia worked to exhaustion. "Sometimes I would come in and Pat would say that I didn't look right, and he would send me home for the day," said Sylvia. "I would take the morning and the afternoon off, get some rest, and then go back at night and have a good practice. I was also bouncing at a local bar before I fought Ricco because I was broke. I don't think I would have made it if it wasn't for Pat, Jeremy, Matt, Robbie, and Jens. They knew I could beat Ricco. My team and I were the only ones in the world who knew I could beat him—nobody else thought I had a chance."

A week prior to the fight, Sylvia flew to Las Vegas to go through his medical examinations and his prefight interviews. Then, on the morning of the show, he suited up in sweatpants, sweatshirt, and a cotton beanie and headed to the MGM Grand auditorium with the rest of his team. "We made sure we were together," said Sylvia. "We went to check out the Octagon, got into the cage, and just talked about the game plan, what I was going to do, how I was going to execute it. Then I ate again and headed backstage. When the fights started, I pretty much stayed in my locker room, pulled my hood up, and tried to stay warm. Jeremy, Matt, and Pat made sure if I needed anything, I got it. They made sure someone was around me at all times, keeping me company. And when the time was near, Pat put on the mitts and we did combinations. Sticking and moving. Then Matt came in and we began to pummel, making sure I got my underhooks in. Then Jeremy put on the sparring gear, and we did a round of sparring. He'd throw kicks, and I had to counter with punches."

Finally, once they got the cue, the entire entourage headed out into the smoke and lights and began the descent toward the Octagon. Jeremy, Matt, and Pat quickly positioned themselves in Sylvia's corner, ready to give him instructions throughout the fight. They would tell him to work his jab. They would make sure he kept his chin down, tell him when to throw the thunderous right hand, and point out any openings they saw. But once Sylvia stepped into the Octagon, it was up to him to bring home the title belt.

Sylvia's mind cleared. One the other side of the Octagon stood Rodriguez, the man everyone expected to win. But when the bout started, Sylvia planted a solid jab into the face of his opponent, showing everyone that he wasn't a chump fighter. Rodriguez backed up, shook his head, and then reevaluated the situation. A few seconds later, he decided that bringing the fight to the ground would be a better approach. "As soon as he shot, I moved and threw him to the side," said Sylvia. "I was like, 'This kid is weak. If this is all he is bringing, he is in trouble.' He shot in again and again, and I kept getting the underhooks and pushing him away. When he came too close, I hit him a couple of times. He shied away because he didn't like it. I thought, 'Sooner or later, I'm going to get a hold of this guy.'"

Rodriguez managed to get Sylvia to the ground several times, but then he had to use all his limbs just to hold him down. This made him vulnerable to strikes, and when he let go of his hold to block punches, Sylvia backed out and stood up. As the fight progressed, Rodriguez started having a harder time getting his mitts on Sylvia, so he decided to step forward and exchange punches. Sylvia had several inches on his reach, however, and his shots began landing right and left. In retaliation, Rodriguez threw a kick, and Sylvia countered with a right hand that missed by inches. Then, just a few moments later, Rodriguez threw yet another kick, and this time Sylvia landed his right flush on his target. "I didn't think it would happen that quick," said Sylvia. "I thought he would be real frustrated at the end of this round, and I was going to come out and put the pressure on him real good. He threw that leg kick, and I threw the right, tagged him a little bit. I thought, 'Please do that again.' He did it again, and I threw that hard right straight down the pipe."

Rocked in the face, Rodriguez fell to the floor. Sylvia followed him down, raining punches. After a few shots had landed, Rodriguez was unconscious, and the referee pulled Sylvia off him. "I forgot that I had just won the belt," said Sylvia. "I was pumped because everyone said I shouldn't have gotten the fight. I was pumped because I had been a five-to-one underdog, and I had won. I jumped up and said, 'What's up now! To hell with all you guys!' All my teammates jumped into the ring to support me, and it was one of the best feelings I ever had. But it wasn't until they wrapped the belt around my waist that I realized what I had done. I had just become the heavyweight champion of the UFC."

Despite Sylvia having just accomplished the most difficult goal of his life, he was at the Miletich Fighting Systems Monday morning rolling around on the mats. He understood that the sport was evolving very fast and that the only way to stay on top of the pile was to never slack, not even for a moment. "For anyone out there thinking about coming to train with us, be prepared to do a lot of hard work," said Sylvia. "It's a lot of hard work, and you have to be very humble. We've had guys who come in here with attitudes—they get all bloodied up and get put to sleep, and they don't come back. So be prepared to face some of the best guys in the world. You have to have an open mind, because we have a lot of animals in that room—a lot of animals people don't even know about. But if you come here with the right attitude and train hard, anything is possible. Anything."

The Final Shot

On November 12, 1993, the first Ultimate Fighting Championship (UFC) brought the martial arts world together for the first time. With submission fighters such as Royce Gracie and Ken Shamrock running through the competition, traditional martial artists began searching for instructors who could teach them the art of ground fighting. While they played catch-up, a host of amateur wrestlers entered the UFC to see how their skills fared. They garnered their share of victories for a time, but it wasn't long before their fellow competitors caught onto their tricks. To remain competitive, the wrestlers began heading to the same schools as the submission fighters and strikers.

Everyone needed one another to keep up. Submission fighters shared their secrets of joint locks and chokeholds. Wrestlers offered their knowledge of takedowns. Strikers revealed the movement and timing behind their punches and kicks. "It was unbelievable how fast you saw everyone lose their traditional styles and begin this process of cross-training," said Dan Severn. "All of a sudden you saw wrestlers who could kick, and strikers could shoot in and take an opponent down."

Because of one groundbreaking event, the martial arts had evolved more in a decade than it had in the thousand years prior. The UFC had given birth to the sport of mixed martial arts (MMA). Competitors shed the "Us vs. Them" mentality, and they bonded together as a family. "Now we all get along, and we really try to take the sport to the next level," said Mark Coleman. "Most of the time you get into the ring with someone you know, but you put that aside to get the win. Afterward, you shake hands—there is no reason we can't be friends. What matters is making the sport go mainstream so we can all make a living and continue to do what we do."

The Zuffa team purchased the UFC with this same goal in mind. In just a few years, they have not only managed to bring the UFC back to worldwide pay-per-view, but they have also educated the public concerning the heart, courage, and skill of every fighter who steps into the Octagon, drawing millions of new fans to the sport. With submission fighters such as BJ Penn catching his victims in joint locks, wrestlers such as Matt Hughes slamming his prey to the canvas, and strikers such as Yves Edwards knocking his opponents out with strikes, the sport of MMA has reached a pinnacle of popularity and talent. Unquestionably, the UFC has finally climbed out of obscurity and into the public eye, and with fighters continuing to refine their skills, there is no telling where the sport will head tomorrow.

Index

NOTE: *Italics* indicate photographs

Author Erich Krauss (right) fighting in Thailand.

About the Author

Erich Krauss began his fighting career in the smoky underground gambling halls of Pataya, Thailand. After numerous amateur bouts and a professional record of 3-0, Krauss brought his fighting back to the United States and is now training at the world-renowned Lion's Den in San Diego, California. Through this association, he has cultivated close personal friendships with both Bob and Ken Shamrock, and developed professional relationships with the top fighters of the mixed martial arts world.

In his latest work, *Into the Octagon*, Erich Krauss chronicles the official history of the Ultimate Fighting Championship and its legends through gripping narrative and action packed fight photographs. Krauss is the author of *Brawl* (ECW Press, 2002), a book that focuses on the history and rise of mixed martial arts competition, which is currently on its third printing, *Little Evil* (ECW Press, 2003), and *On the Line: Inside the U.S. Border Patrol* (Citadel Press, 2004). He is also the author of the forthcoming books *Martial Arts Unleashed: Jiu-Jitsu* (McGraw Hill, 2004), *Wall of Flame: The Heroic Battle to Save Southern California* (Wiley, 2005), and *Beyond the Lion's Den* (Tuttle, 2005). He lives in San Diego, California.

Ultimate Knockout 1 & 2 Combo—On Sale Now

For the FIRST TIME EVER, UFCs Ultimate Knockouts 1&2 are available on one Double Feature Disc!

Featuring OVER 40 of the best knockouts in Ultimate Fighting Championship's History from 1993 to 2002!

All of the UFC stars from past and present are featured, including: TITO ORTIZ, CHUCK LIDDELL, PHIL BARONI, TANK ABBOTT, RANDY COUTURE, VICTOR BELFORT, MARK WEIR, CAOL UNO, ROBBIE LAWLER, MATT HUGHES, PEDRO RIZZO AND MORE!

DVD special features include: All Event Fights, Spanish commentary, Behind the Scene Action, & Ultimate Music.

UFC 43: Meltdown—On Sale Now

UFC is back in blistering Las Vegas at the Thomas & Mack Center for UFC 43: Meltdown.

In the main event, Light Heavyweight number-one contender Chuck "The Iceman" Liddell battles two-time former UFC Heavyweight Champion Randy "The Natural" Couture for the Interim Light Heavyweight Championship.

The undercard is stacked with such UFC stars as Tank Abbott, Kimo, Vitor Belfort, Frank Mir, Yves Edwards, and Ian Freeman.

DVD special features include: All Event Fights, Spanish commentary, Behind the Scene Action, & Ultimate Music.

Side #1—

1. Randy Couture Makes Weight [1:13]
2. Yves Edwards Makes Weight [1:02]
3. Vitor Belfort Makes Weight [1:04]
4. Ken Shamrock at the Weigh-In [2:49]
5. No Love Lost Between Wes Sims and Tim Sylvia [1:19]
6. Pedro Rizzo and Tra Telligman Enter the Octagon [:56]

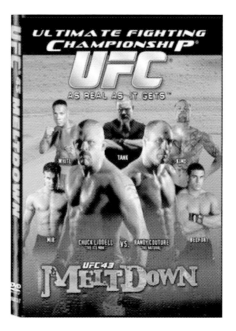

7. Pedro Rizzo Post Fight [1:14]
8. Frank Mir and Wes Sims Enter the Octagon [1:32]
9. Frank Mir has a Few Words for Wes Sims [1:49]
10. Vernon "Tiger" White Pre-Fight [1:56]
11. Kimo and Tank Pre-Fight [1:26]
12. Kimo Post Fight [:34]
13. Couture and Liddell Prepare to Fight [4:28]
14. Vitor Belfort Post-Fight [:50]
15. Randy Couture Post-Fight [2:12]
2. Pedro Rizzo vs. Tra Telligman (Prelim) [12:48]
3. Matt Lindland vs. Falaniko Vitale (Prelim) [2:41]
4. Yves Edwards vs. Eddie Ruiz (Prelim) [18:34]
5. Frank Mir vs. Wes Sims [11:03]
6. Ian Freeman vs. Vernon White [18:27]
7. Vitor Belfort vs. Marvin Eastman [6:57]
8. Tank Abbott vs. Kimo Leopoldo [5:55]
9. Chuck Liddell vs. Randy Couture [19:25]
10. Play All [30:20]

UFC 44: Undisputed—On Sale Now

The UFC returns to the Mandalay Bay Events Center in Las Vegas for UFC 44: Undisputed.

In the main event, Light Heavyweight Champion Tito Ortiz takes on Interim Light Heavy Champion Randy Couture for the Undisputed Light Heavyweight Championship.

The co-main event is a battle of giants as 6'8" 265 pound UFC Champion Tim Sylvia defends his title against 6'10", 265 pound challenge Gan McGee.

The undercard features such rising UFC stars as Rich Franklin, Andrei Arlovski, Hermes Franca, and Josh Thomson. A total of 9 fights.

DVD special features include: All Event Fights, Spanish commentary, Behind the Scene Action, & Ultimate Music.

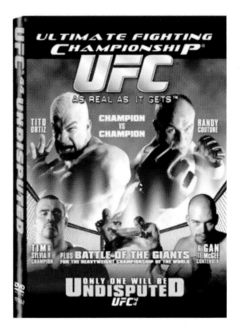

Side #1—

1 Rich Franklin Makes Weight [1:23]
2. Tito and Randy Square Off at the Weigh-In [2:48]
3. "The Crow" Weighs in Over the Limit [:48]
4. Tim Sylvia Must Make Weight a Second Time [:45]
5. Rich Franklin and Edwin Dewees Prepare to Face Off [1:27]
6. Hermes Franca Post Fight [1:17]
7. Battle of the Giants [3:26]
8. Tim Sylvia Post Fight [:53]
9. Tito Ortiz and Randy Couture Prep for Battle [2:54]
10. Randy Couture Post Fight [1:43]
2. Caol Uno vs Hermes Franca (Prelim) [3:05]
3. (Prelim) Jeremy Jackson vs. Nick Diaz [9:49]
4. Josh Thomson vs. Gerald Strebendt (Prelim) [15:31]
5. Dave Strasser vs. Karo Parisyan (Prelim) [3:38]
6. Rich Franklin vs. Edwin Dewees [4:52]
7. David Loiseau vs. Jorge Rivera [4:44]
8. Tim Sylvia vs. Gan McGee [19:58]

10. Andrei Arlovski vs. Vladimir Matyushenko [9:51]
11. Tito Ortiz vs. Randy Couture [4:22]

UFC 45: Revolution—On Sale Now

The premier mixed martial arts event in the world returns to the Mohegan Sun Arena for its 10th Anniversary at UFC 45: Revolution.

In the main event, Welterweight Champion Matt Hughes defends his belt against top-ranked contender Frank Trigg in a grudge match two years in the making.

The co-main event is a battle of big punchers as UFC legend Tank Abbott takes on young brawler Cabbage Correira.

Fight Card

Matt Hughes vs. Frank Trigg
Evan Tanner vs. Phil Baroni
Wesley Correira vs. David Abbott
Yves Edwards vs. Nick Agallar
Keith Rockel vs. Chris Liguori
Pedro Rizzo vs. Ricco Rodriguez
Robbie Lawler vs. Chris Lytle
Matt Lindland vs. Falaniko Vitale

Features

DVD special features include: All Event Fights, Spanish commentary, Behind the Scene Action, & Ultimate Music.

Contains special ceremony marking the 10th anniversary of the UFC including legendary fighters Royce Gracie and Ken Shamrock's induction as the charter members of the new UFC Hall of Fame!

Side #1—
1. 10 Years of the UFC [3:02]
2. UFC Legends Autograph Session [1:01]
3. Phil Baroni Walks to the Arena With His Team [:59]
4. Baroni and Tanner Showdown [3:47]
5. Robbie Lawler Post Fight [1:22]
6. Tank and Cabbage Prepare for War [1:45]
7. Tank and Cabbage Post Fight Reactions [1:05]
8. Hughes and Trigg Prepare for War [3:22]
9. Matt Hughes Post Fight [1:26]
10. Viewers Choice Awards [19:13]
1. Event Opening [1:32]
2. Yves Edwards vs. Nick Agallar (Prelim) [8:56]
3. Keith Rockel vs. Chris Liguori (Premlim) [4:57]
4. Ricco Rodriguez vs. Pedro Rizzo (Prelim) [18:16]
5. Robbie Lawler vs. Chris Lytle [22:52]
6. Phil Baroni vs. Evan Tanner [10:30]
7. Tank Abbott vs. "Cabbage" [6:37]
8. Falaniko Vitale vs. Matt Lindland [5:51]
9. Matt Huges vs. Frank Trigg [27:51]

UFC 46: Supernatural—On Sale Now

JANUARY 31, 2004 The premier mixed martial arts event in the world returns to Las Vegas on Super Saturday for UFC 46: Supernatural.

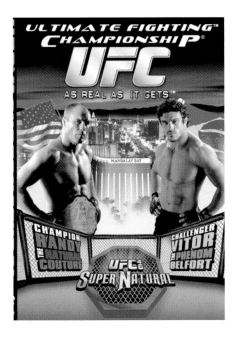

In the main event, Light Heavyweight Champion Randy "The Natural" Couture puts his belt on the line in a rematch against Brazil's Vitor "The Phenom" Belfort.

The co-main event features the top lightweight, BJ Penn, moving up in weight to challenge five-time defending champion Matt Hughes for his Welterweight belt. The undercard features such UFC stars as Frank Mir, Carlos Newton, Lee Murray, Josh Thomson, Hermes Franca and Charuto Verissimo rounding out the even!

DVD special features include: All Event Fights, Spanish commentary, Behind the Scene Action, & Ultimate Music.

Side #1—
1. Chuck and Tito UFC 47 Faceoff [1:35]
2. Frank Mir vs. Wes Sims: Grudge Match [3:56]
3. Lee Murray and Jorge Rivera Prepare for Battle [3:07]
4. Lee Murray Post Fight [1:13]
5. BJ Penn and Mat Hughes: Power vs. Speed [3:00]

6. BJ Penn Post Fight [1:59]
7. BJ Penn Watches His Teacher Fight [1:09]
8. Randy Couture vs. Vitor Belfort Super Natural [2:40]
9. Vitor Belfort Post Fight [1:39]
1. Jeff Curran vs. Matt Serra (Prelim) [:22]
2. (Prelim) Josh Thomson vs. Hermes Franca [16:51]
3. Georges St. Pierre vs. Karo Parisyan (Prelim) [16:48]
4. Lee Murray vs. Jorge Rivera [17:28]
5. Wes Sims vs. Frank Mir [3:03]
6. B.J. Penn vs. Matt Hughes [10:39]
7. Renato Verissimo vs. Carlos Newton [2:20]
8. Vitor Belfort vs. Randy Couture [14:18]

UFC 47: It's On—On Sale Now

Tito Ortiz vs. Chuck Liddell
Wesley "Cabbage" Correira vs. Andrei Arlovski
Mike Kyle vs. Wes Sims
Jonathan Wiezorek vs.Wade Shipp
Robbie Lawler vs. Nick Diaz
Chris Lytle vs. Tiki Ghosen
Yves Edwards vs. Hermes Franca
Mike Brown vs. Genki Sudo

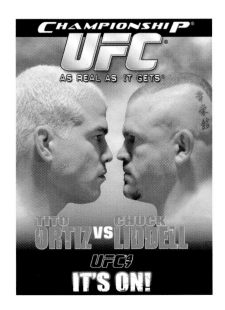

UFC 48: Payback—Release Dec 14, 2004

Ken Shamrock vs. Kimo

Tim Sylvia vs. Frank Mir

Matt Hughes vs. Renato Verissimo

Phil Baroni vs. Evan Tanner

Trevor Prangley vs. Curtis Stout

Dennis Hallman vs. Frank Trigg

Matt Serra vs. Ivan Menjivar

Georges St. Pierre vs. Jay Hieron

Music CD: Ultimate Beatdowns Vol. 1 Metal— On sale Now

NITRUS/DRT TO RELEASE ULTIMATE FIGHT-ING CHAMPIONSHIP COMPILATION

Ultimate Beatdowns Vol. 1 Metal in-stores August 24

New York, NY—Nitrus/DRT will release the metal compilation album Ultimate Fighting Championship Ultimate Beatdowns Vol. 1. The album is due in-stores on August 24.

Ultimate Beatdowns is the first collection to be released in conjunction with the UFC. The UFC is a highly intense and popular combat sport. The UFC is defined as a Mixed Martial Arts competition between highly skilled professional fighters who utilize the disciplines of Jiu-Jitsu, Karate, Boxing, Kickboxing, Wrestling and other forms of fighting in live events. "Ultimate Fighters" are among the best-trained and conditioned athletes in the world.

Ultimate Beatdowns is the perfect companion to the sport's high energy and intensity it generates. The album features 15 new and unreleased tracks from Sepultura, Hatebreed, Slayer, Damageplan and American Head Charge, among others.

The Ultimate Beatdowns track listing:

"Warzone," Slayer

"Blunt Force Trauma," Damageplan

"Live for This," Hatebreed

"Bullet the Blue Sky," Sepultura

"Indifferent to Suffering," Chimaira

"Born to Crush You," Icepick (featuring Jamey Jasta of Hatebreed)

"The Mob Goes Wild," Clutch

"Cowards," American Head Charge

"Breathe Life," Killswitch Engage

"It's Alright," U.P.O.

"Face the Pain," Stemm

"Dying Here," Scars of Life

"Lost Cause," Black Flood Diesel

"Power of I and I," Shadows Fall